I've Got *My Joy* Back

I've Got My Joy Back

With God you can regain your joy, no matter how tough your circumstances may be.

An inspirational guide to finding joy again through God and Jesus Christ using scripture and a minister's instructional testimony about overcoming grief and depression.

Dr. Cassandra Altenor, Th.D

XULON PRESS

Xulon Press
2301 Lucien Way #415
Maitland, FL 32751
407.339.4217
www.xulonpress.com

© 2021 by Dr. Cassandra Altenor, Th.D

Photographer: Victoria J Smith
Editors: Nancy N. Alexander and Rose E. Dextra

All rights reserved solely by the author. The author guarantees all contents are original and do not infringe upon the legal rights of any other person or work. No part of this book may be reproduced in any form without the permission of the author. The views expressed in this book are not necessarily those of the publisher. Due to the changing nature of the Internet, if there are any web addresses, links, or URLs included in this manuscript, these may have been altered and may no longer be accessible. The views and opinions shared in this book belong solely to the author and do not necessarily reflect those of the publisher. The publisher therefore disclaims responsibility for the views or opinions expressed within the work.

Unless otherwise indicated, Scripture quotations taken from the King James Version (KJV) – public domain.

Scripture quotations taken from the New King James Version (NKJV). Copyright © 1982 by Thomas Nelson, Inc. Used by permission. All rights reserved.

Scripture quotations taken from the Holy Bible, New International Version (NIV). Copyright © 1973, 1978, 1984, 2011 by Biblica, Inc.™. Used by permission. All rights reserved.

Scripture quotations taken from the English Standard Version (ESV). Copyright © 2001 by Crossway, a publishing ministry of Good News Publishers. Used by permission. All rights reserved.

Scripture quotations taken from the Amplified Bible (AMP). Copyright © 1954, 1958, 1962, 1964, 1965, 1987 by The Lockman Foundation. Used by permission. All rights reserved.

Paperback ISBN-13: 978-1-6628-1739-7
Hard Cover ISBN-13: 978-1-6628-1740-3
Ebook ISBN-13: 978-1-6628-1741-0

Table of Contents

Introduction ix
Chapter 1: How Did I Get Here? 1
Chapter 2: True Joy. 43
Chapter 3: I Choose Joy. 54
Chapter 4: Accepting God's Love 64
Chapter 5: Steps to Your Deliverance. 72
Chapter 6: Scared, but Do It Anyway! 98
Chapter 7: Don't Get Bitter—Get Better 114
Chapter 8: You Have Nothing to Lose. 142
Chapter 9: Use Your Toolbox. 163
Chapter 10: Jesus Will Give You Beauty for Your Ashes. . . . 183
Chapter 11: Don't Quit on Your Joy 203

Dedication

First, I would like to give thanks to God for allowing me to write this book. I would like to dedicate this book to my beloved Pastor Rev. Dr. Jacqueline Waite for being my Pastor, and my mentor and confidant. To my mother thank you for bringing me into this world and showing me a great example of what it means to have courage and endurance during tough times; to my beloved sister Stephanie for never giving up on me; and family for always supporting me. To my church family, thank you for all your prayers. Finally, my son Will, you are a special blessing to me, and you bring me so much joy I thank God for you. Love you everyone.

Introduction

This book is dedicated to you. Yes, you.

If you've been feeling like your life is in a rut, you've lost your joy, your passion, your peace of mind, and you are feeling like you're stuck in a pit, this book is for you.

Please don't be discouraged—you're not the only one feeling this way. So many people lack this great treasure called joy. In the book of Nehemiah 8:10, the word of the Lord says, "That the joy of the Lord is your strength."

I am here to let you know that if you've lost your joy, you can get it back through a life yielded to the Holy Spirit and living in His word. I know that sometimes you may feel helpless, as if you are stuck in a dark place. But there is a light that shines through every dark crevice of your soul and in every situation that you face each day: King Jesus.

You need to know that there is a place that you will reach in your life that is so broken and dark, and only the light of Jesus can guide you out. Close to twenty years ago, you see, I was living as if nothing mattered. I partied and got high because I was broken and sad on the inside. I was looking for love in all the wrong places. I was living a life that was filled with disappointments. But one Monday night, I was invited to a prayer meeting. I wasn't invited directly but I went out of curiosity—or so I thought. It was God's master plan. I was even shocked that I said yes.

On the way to the prayer meeting, I kept on telling myself, "Cassie, what are you really doing here? Are you serious? This is just going to be a waste of your time." Oh, boy. Was I wrong! Well, I walked into this house, which back in the day was the house where we would cut school, hang out, and have house parties. Now, I was thinking in my mind, "These jokers are saying that they are having a prayer meeting. What a joke!"

From the moment I stepped into the room, something gripped me. The atmosphere felt different—nothing like I have ever felt before. Then the saints started to pray. I don't even think there are words adequate to describe what took place that night. The joke was on me.

To this day, I can't remember a word from those prayers, but I will never forget how those prayers made me feel. The presence of God was so rich in that little living room that I literally felt that God had stripped me of my shame, my insecurities, low self-esteem and anxiety issues, abandonment issues, all of which I became an expert at hiding from myself and others. I thought I was in control. Then, I felt a warmth that overwhelmed me: I felt the love of Jesus and His grace embrace me. As it was happening, I felt as though I was having an out-of-body experience because I was saying to myself, "Cassie, what is happening to you? Do you realize that you are breaking down in front of these people? What are you doing?" I just didn't care anymore; I didn't want the feeling to stop. I felt like a big weight was lifted off from my body. I felt freedom.

God came down and raised me and I surrendered; my heart fell prostrate at His feet. I just started to weep uncontrollably and as I cried; I began to feel lighter. The more I wept, the lighter I felt.

I left different and embarrassed, but the thing that I knew is that I needed more of that. I didn't realize that it was the working of the Holy Spirit—I just knew that I needed more! God's love was simply irresistible to me. God is so funny in the way that He orchestrates our lives. My life was changed for good that very night, and I finally experienced what true joy was. The walls that I worked hard to build around my heart after my father walked out of my life all came tumbling down with just one touch of His glory.

I have discovered that through some of the roughest times of my life that Jesus has always been there for me in my darkest hours and brightest days; He truly is my only hope. God makes no mistakes. He cannot lie and He never fails. You see, the truth is that you were designed by God for greatness.

Sometimes it feels as though the situations or predicaments we find ourselves in, are undeserving of His love. He delights in us and loves us despite it all. I've asked myself several times, "How can an amazing God love me with all the bad decisions that I've made in the past?" Then I remind myself that His word assures us that His grace is sufficient for all of us. The Apostle Paul said in II Corinthians 12:9, "And he said unto me, my grace is sufficient for thee: for my strength is made perfect in weakness. Most gladly, therefore, will I rather glory in my infirmities, that the power of Christ may rest upon me." When we are weak, He is strong. I believe that we work too hard on trying to convince people that we are strong when, in our weakness, God gets the most glory and is able to show His amazing strength toward His children.

God is concerned about His children being whole, which includes our body, mind, and spirit. The time that we spend at church during our weekly services makes us feel good for the moment. But after that, we go through our week, sometimes feeling unfulfilled, defeated, and sometimes overwhelmed with the battles of life.

Trust me, I know it is a daily struggle for us to maintain our joy as believers. I can only imagine how hard it must be if you're someone that is living in this dark, dying world without Jesus Christ. People search for joy and peace through their careers, alcohol, social media, or the approval of others—but they never find them. Well, it's all in King Jesus. Every peace that you could ever imagine having is in Christ Jesus.

The war is on and the enemy has intensified his strategies and tactics to keep us in bondage through oppression, disappointment, rejection, depression, mind games, and most importantly, getting us off the path toward our divine destiny. The enemy is after our mind because he knows that our mind is where the battlefield is. The word of God says in Ephesians 6:12, "For we wrestle not against flesh and blood, but against principalities, against powers, against the rulers of the darkness of this world, against spiritual wickedness in high places." The warfare is real!

Have you ever felt disoriented, worried, anxious, or frustrated? Well, if you haven't, I am here to confess that I've been there. Now that I think about it, I think that if you have lived on Earth for more than fifteen to sixteen years, then you must have experienced some sort of disappointment, rejection, or a sense of hopelessness.

There is a place that you go when you are feeling all alone, hopeless, weak, disappointed, and battered. It's considered to be a dark place, a place of shame, confusion, and anxiety. It's the place where you go in your mind and it brings back all the painful memories, regrets, and failures. It's the place where you find yourself feeling overwhelmed with the cares of this life, struggling with grief and unexpected loss, sickness, or perhaps a divorce. I think we've all been to this place, don't you?

Nothing in life but the word of God can prepare you for the survival skills that are needed for the low seasons we all will be faced with in this journey called life. Every crisis, disappointment, grief, and challenge that you are being faced with has already been conquered on Calvary when Jesus died on the cross. Your hope and answer is Jesus Christ. Believe and trust in Him for He is the way. There is not enough money in the world, not a house big enough, not enough cars, or any vacation that will give us more everlasting peace than the Lord. Without Jesus, we can never have true peace nor joy.

So, what do you do when the enemy is trying to fill your heart with unforgiveness, resentment, doubt, fear, and anxiety? What do you do when you feel all alone at the worst time of your life? What do you do when you feel misunderstood?

When you feel as if you have been knocked down to the ground, all you need to do is to look up and not to the sky but to the One who made Heaven and Earth: God, our Prince of Peace. The book of Psalms 91:1 says, "He that dwelleth in the secret place of the most-High shall abide under the shadow of the Almighty." In that secret place, it's just you and God, no loved ones nor your haters are there. When you abide in God, you feel joy and peace.

There is a place where you completely surrender your will, and all the superficial things don't matter. All that is important is God's presence. There is a place where you are left to look in the mirror and admit that it is the real you and that it is not as pretty as you've worked so hard to make everyone believe it to be. At that place, you are faced with the truth that you do have some insecurities, fears, anxiety, damaging thoughts, and perceptions of ourselves. That place is where the self is crushed and slain, where nothing matters but God's presence. We, as children of God, have been given access to the Kingdom of Heaven, where we can connect and get divine healing and breakthrough. It is at that place that you will find your hope and joy in an everlasting and never-failing Father.

To go to that secret place, you must learn how to tap into that supernatural, never-failing source called joy. You see, through the Holy Spirit, we have access to the fountain of living water. You may feel like you are in a barren place with no growth, a deserted place, but the word of God says in John 7:38, "He that believeth in me, as the scripture had said, out of his belly shall flow rivers of living water." Jesus is that fountain of living water that will quench every thirst and provide wells in every desert of your life.

A yearning for something more in life is usually the Holy Spirit trying to get your attention because He desires to dwell in you and be your Father. You may feel that you don't have support around you to get you to that special place. Well, I am here to encourage you to know that you *can* make it without all the things the enemy has told you that you are lacking. So, walk in victory with your head high and know that Jesus Christ paid the price for you to have everlasting joy.

Whatever situation you are in, you can hit reset, you can recalculate, you can start over, you can have a new beginning, and you can start a new chapter in your life called Joy. It is possible to live a life filled with joy and peace through the atoning blood of our Lord Jesus Christ. Once you have given your life to Jesus, there is a treasure called joy that is downloaded in every believer. The scriptures say in II Corinthians 4:7, "But we have this treasure in earthen vessels, that the Excellency of the power may be of God, and not of us."

There is a treasure inside of you and one of the pieces of that treasure is called joy. To rebound from the challenges in your life, you need to rediscover this joy and explore it through the word of God. In this book, you will see some of my personal struggles that I faced and overcame. I will share with you what it means to have the joy of the Lord in your heart as well as give you steps on how to get your deliverance and triumph. You will also find some tools that you can use when you are facing a difficult season and some references to people who also faced extreme challenges but were able to persevere and have joy. Most importantly, you will see the word of God throughout the entire book, which I believe is the most powerful tool that you could own.

I pray that this book will give you some tools for you to get your joy back or how to keep your peace that can only be received from God.

Chapter 1:
How Did I Get Here?

Do you remember when it started? I am sure you are trying to figure out what in the world I am talking about. Do you remember the first day you started to feel so overwhelmed that you couldn't get out of bed? The first day you stopped laughing, or the day the enemy started taking your smile away?

Well, of course not. You probably can't remember because depression happens gradually. It's important to know that not all periods of sadness are depression—all of us have gone through a season of pain and unhappiness. We may be sad because we are grieving for a lost loved one because we are finding out that we may have cancer or a chronic disease, or because we're just going through a time of uncertainty. Depression is defined by the National Institute of Mental Health as a "common but serious mood disorder." It causes severe symptoms that affect how you feel, think, and handle daily activities, such as sleeping, eating, or working. To be diagnosed with depression, the symptoms must be present for at least two weeks."[1] There are many different types of depression with varying intensities, which include persistent depressive disorder, postpartum depression, psychotic depression, seasonal affective disorder, bipolar disorder, and more.

As a child of God, I know that depression is a spirit of the devil: the word of God says in ²John 10:10, "The thief cometh not, but for to steal, and to kill, and to destroy, I have come that they might have life and that they might have it more abundantly." Depression comes to steal our joy and rob us of our peace. Depression is a spirit of the enemy that has a way of just getting us emotionally and mentally stuck. It comes to drain the life out of you. Most people don't just wake up one day depressed for no apparent reason, but some things trigger us that are associated with trauma. The spirit of depression usually occurs after a negative event or a series of negative events in our lives. Sometimes we are just dealt with some difficult circumstances and conditions, such as cancer or a loss of a loved one and this is why we need Jesus in our lives, because He is the only one that is able to keep us in those moments.

Often times people are just dropped, and you will understand what I mean shortly. Betrayal, unforgiveness, strife, all of these can lead to depression. There was a man in the Bible called Mephibosheth. According to the biblical narrative ³(2 Samuel 4:4), Mephibosheth was five years old when both his father and grandfather died at the Battle of Mount Gilboa. After the deaths of Saul and Jonathan, Mephibosheth's nurse took him and fled in panic. In her haste, the child fell, or was dropped while fleeing. Mephibosheth was crippled in both feet and he had no control over these negative events which took place early in his life. Although most of us haven't been physically dropped by someone which caused us to become crippled, but for some reason or another we have been wounded, hurt and crippled, emotionally, spiritually and psychologically. How many of us have gotten dropped by a failed marriage, betrayal of a friend or a mate, by our jobs. Being dropped can simply mean that we were leaning and counting on someone who failed us and dropped us emotionally and we carry that pain which weighs us down, but Jesus wants to heal you from that drop. It's interesting to note that when I researched Mephibosheth's name in the Bible dictionary, it meant "from the mouth of shame". Wow, even his name was associated with sad, he had everything stacked up against him, but God delivered him from his depression and his misery. He was mentally at a place of depression and even his physical location was depressing. The Bible stated that he came from a place called Lo-debar. I learned that Lo-debar was a town in Gilead in (2 Samuel 9:4-5) in ancient Israel. The meaning of Lo-debar meant no communication, no pasture and no word. How ironic because this man was depressed and alone and this all makes sense how he ended up in a place where there was no communication. The way out of Lo-debar is submission and obedience. We must understand that enemy is very crafty and cunning, so we have to always be mindful of our thoughts, our words and our locations. Never stay at a place of sadness, depression, bitterness, unforgiveness, and doubt too long: that is not to say each of us hasn't been there, but go through it and never park there. The enemy is constantly trying to get us to become isolated when we are depressed so he could fill our minds with lies. But you see at the end of his story God used King David to restore the joy of his salvation. This story shows us that it's always good to be kind and good to people when you can or have the power to do so. David remembered Jonathan's kindness. David thought about Jonathan and the promise that he made to him and wanted to show Saul's family kindness because of his love for Johnathan who later died in war. David sent his servant Ziba to find Mephibosheth, and when Ziba returned to David, he told him that he'd found Mephibosheth, but he is crippled. The world and man see's our weakness, our failure and our condition but God sees it as an opportunity to perform a miracle in your life. David was determined to honor his promise to his friend, so he called Miphiboseth. Even after they found him, and he needed someone to carry him and sometimes you will be at a place where you need someone to lift you up in prayer and lift you up with encouraging words and sometimes just a hug. After meeting David, Mephibosheth still felt unqualified not deserving any honor. There is a lady in my church named Sis Christine who always makes this statement in her prayers, "God did not choose the qualified, but he qualifies the called". David told Mephibosheth no that I promised your father that I would always take care of you. Other people have taken the land that belonged to Saul and Jonathan and your family. I will now give all of it back to you. Also, I would like to make a special place at my table for you. Anytime you want to come and eat with me or visit me at the palace you can come. You will never have to worry about anything because I will always take care of you. Isn't that amazing David took away the shame and rejection which he probably experienced for most of his life. God is here to give you the same restoration in your life. God desires to lift us up out of our dark places and deliver us from anything that binds us and deliver us from bondage. I pray today that everything that has made you feel less than, not qualified, inferior, disenfranchised, not good enough, that the fire of God will consume all of the wicked lies of the enemy and you will know that you are a son and daughter of the King. My dear brother in the Lord Deacon Evans recently preached a sound word and the message was "You're God's Masterpiece". It is my desire that you will truly understand and get the revelation how much God truly loves you.

    I used to think that because I am a Christian, I can't possibly suffer from depression. It is a spirit that attacks God's children. This spirit can lay dormant and tries to attack every last one of us. You don't have to be embarrassed or ashamed if you are suffering from depression because Jesus Christ can set you free. Sometimes, depending on your cultural background, men are noted to be strong and don't like to be associated with having mental issues. But depression is not a male or a female problem; it's a humanity problem.

I remember the time when the enemy attacked me with the spirit of depression. I didn't even realize it. I didn't know the signs nor could ever think that I could experience this demonic spirit in my life. [4]According to the National Institute of Mental Health, if you have been experiencing some of the following signs and symptoms most of the day for at least two weeks, you may be suffering from depression:

- Persistent sadness, anxious, or "empty" mood
- Feelings of hopelessness, or pessimism
- Irritability
- Feelings of guilt, worthlessness, or helplessness
- Loss of interest or pleasure in hobbies and activities
- Decreased energy or fatigue
- Moving or talking more slowly
- Feeling restless or having trouble sitting still
- Difficulty concentrating, remembering, or making decisions
- Difficulty sleeping, early-morning awakening, or oversleeping
- Appetite and/or weight changes
- Thoughts of death, or suicide attempts
- Aches or pains, headaches, cramps, or digestive problems without a clear physical cause that do not ease even with treatment

Not everyone who is depressed experiences every symptom. Some people experience only a few symptoms, while others may experience many. Several persistent symptoms in addition to low mood are required for a diagnosis of major depression, but people with only a few—but distressing—symptoms may benefit from the treatment of their "subsyndromal" depression. The severity and frequency of the symptoms and how long they last vary depending on the individual and his or her particular illness. Symptoms may also vary depending on the stage of the illness.

I didn't even think that I could go through such a low state. I felt like I was experiencing spiritual quicksand; everything around me was pulling me in. I felt an overcast of depression that was hovering over my life. I didn't have a moment when the enemy wasn't attacking me in every direction. Whether it was psychological, physical, emotional, or spiritual, it was clear that the enemy had unleashed all his ammunition to try to destroy my life.

But the devil is a liar. God delivered me from that bondage and spirit of depression, and He gave me back my joy and peace. It didn't happen overnight, but it happened—the chains were broken, and my joy was restored through the blood of Jesus Christ. The word of God states in II Corinthians 10:4-5, "(For the weapons of our warfare are not carnal, but mighty through God to the pulling down of strong holds;) Casting down imaginations, and every high thing that exalteth itself against the knowledge of God and bringing into captivity every thought to the obedience of Christ;⁵" We have the power through God to destroy every plot of the enemy against our minds. The Holy Spirit had to fortify my mind and granted me deliverance from the spirit of depression and oppression. No matter what it looks like in the natural world, God is working it out where it counts: the realm of the Spirit. God has the power to shift our thoughts, to restore, and to heal us.

Needless to say, I was going through one of the darkest seasons of traumatic events in my life. I was struggling with the spirit of depression and oppression, and the enemy came to test my faith during this season. I was experiencing countless trials and losses. I was extremely unhappy at work and I knew that this job wasn't what I wanted to do for God. I was battling sickness. I suddenly lost my youngest sister and then, then my grandmother, and a few years later, I tragically lost my aunt who was like my mom. I believe that I lost a total of eight people in my life in a course of five years. I felt as if I was losing a part of my heart every time I had to go through another loss. I kept on keeping myself busy, blocking the deaths from my mind, and never really dealt with grieving. I knew that I was not feeling myself, mentally, emotionally, nor physically. I was feeling more sadness and pain than joy and happiness—but I didn't know what to call it. I am a very sociable person and enjoy being around people, but I found myself wanting to be by myself and isolated. It came to a point where I hardly wanted to be around my friends and loved ones. I know that the enemy will use isolation to try to get you all alone to whisper his lies in your mind, but just note that he can never tell you truth all he can feed you with is lies. Just remember the word of God says in [6]John 10:27-28 "My sheep hear my voice, and I know them, and they follow me: And I give unto them eternal life; and they shall never perish, neither shall any man pluck them out of my hand."

Sometimes you may be suffering from the spirit of depression, rejection, or struggling with the spirit of fear, shame and condemnation. Another scriptures that helped me with these spirits of depression and oppression and it was [7]Isaiah 41:10 "Fear thou not; for I am with thee: be not dismayed; for I am thy God: I will strengthen thee; yea, I will help thee; yea, I will uphold thee with the right hand of my righteousness."[8] It is so important to know that the Lord is with you. Although the enemy wants us to feel that we are in this world by ourselves, but our Savior is with us. Life comes with a lot of disappointments, and a couple of "no's" and a few failing seasons, but the Lord is able. As long as you know that you are not where you work, who you are married to, how much you have in your bank, 401K, or where you graduated from, but you are who God say's that you are. The Bible says in the book of ⁹Jeremiah says 1:5 "Before I formed thee in the belly I knew thee; and before thou camest forth out of the womb I sanctified thee, *and* I ordained thee a prophet unto the nations." All that means is that before you mother and your father ever met, God knew that that you would be alive in this time, and in this space for His purpose.

Although you may fail, and you may fall, God still loves you. His love never fails. You can be comforted in your hearts and know that the word of God says in Psalms 30:5 "For his anger endureth but a moment; in his favour is life: weeping may endure for a night but joy cometh in the morning." The ending of this scripture is saying that although you are going through your night season and storm, joy is still coming. Just hold on because morning is coming! The Bible says II Corinthians 4:7, "But we have this treasure in earthen vessels, that the excellency of the power may be of God, and not of us." In other words, we are not living by ourselves; we have the Holy Spirit that abides within us and when we are in the dark valleys or dark corners of life, we can still have joy. The songwriter says that it is in the valley He restores our souls. Isn't it a shame that sometimes it takes us our whole lifetime for us to realize that we are carrying a treasure within us once we have told Jesus yes? You see that treasure wasn't designed to shine when everything is going well. That treasure was designed to shine when everyone has given up on you, when the enemy is telling you that you're not going to be healed, when you have to receive a bad doctor's report, or when you find out that this job that you have dedicated your life to is about to lay you off. Yes, this is exactly when this treasure begins to shine; it is called the glory of God.

I've also asked God in the past, "Where are you?" Sometimes you may feel that you're going through the storm by yourself. Although I knew that I had a relationship with God, I felt that sometimes I couldn't hear His voice. All I could hear was the enemy trying to fill my mind with lies. The spirit of depression was working overtime in my life. I knew that I wasn't myself, so I just stayed in prayer. Sometimes, I felt like I couldn't hear God's voice, but I still believed that He was there. It is in those sorrowful seasons we think that He is not speaking, but that is when I believe that God speaks with volume. You are not alone!

Even though you are a Christian, you are not exempt from the storms of life. You will not go through life without facing a storm. Life will give us some storms that we didn't expect—storms that will knock the wind out of us. In the book of Matthew and Mark we see that Jesus calls the disciples to go into the ship, and in the middle of the night, they experienced a great storm.

We read that the disciples were obedient and followed Jesus, but they still experienced a storm. Jesus was in the ship with them, but they still experienced a storm. Just remember that Jesus is always on the ship, whether you see Him or feel Him, His word is true, and you can be guaranteed that He will show up! The enemy will use different storms to test your faith, relentless in his mission to bring us down and steal our joy and peace of mind. The enemy is doing all he can to find any little crack in your soul. Yes, depression is a spirit straight from hell because the devil's assignment is to get you isolated then eliminate you. Yes, the spirit of depression tries to get you away from your loved ones, away from your friends, derail you from your destiny by speaking lies to your mind—until you begin to speak the lies to yourself, which will, in turn, make you lose your joy. One of the other things that brings depression is pressure and the high demands of life, and since we can't avoid life, we have to tap into the source that will get us not only through life but also allows us to live victoriously. This source that I am referring to is Jesus. The word of the Lord said in 1 John 4:4, "Ye are of God, little children, and have overcome them: because greater is He that is in you, than He that is in the world." God is the only one who could take us through the pressures of life.

Jesus is the hope of glory. I lost my joy, but it was the word of God and prayer that helped me overcome this spirit. Jesus has the power to calm every storm in your life. The Bible says that there was a storm and Jesus was at the bottom of the ship. In the book of Mark, His disciples was very fearful, but Jesus was sleeping.

Mark 4:35-41
[10] "And there arose a great storm of wind, and the waves beat into the ship, so that it was now full. And he was in the hinder part of the ship, asleep on a pillow: and they awake him, and say unto him, Master, carest thou not that we perish? And he arose, and rebuked the wind, and said unto the sea, Peace, be still. And the wind ceased, and there was a great calm. And he said unto them, why are ye so fearful? how is it that ye have no faith? And they feared exceedingly, and said one to another, what manner of man is this, that even the wind and the sea obey him?"

The word of God said that Jesus spoke to the wind, Jesus said, peace, be still. When God speaks a word in your life, your life will never be the same. Jesus wants us to have peace and joy. God can deliver us from our trial, but we must learn that He is also able to sustain us through tough times.

Well, there is a famous story in the Old Testament about a prophet named Elijah—a man that was chosen by God to be the game-changer of his time. Elijah defended the worship of the true and holy God over the false Canaanite deity Baal. [11]God also used Elijah to perform many miracles including raising the dead, bringing fire down from the sky, and entering heaven alive "by fire." Elijah was very powerful. His assignment was not an easy one, and it was an assignment that came with a lot of pressure. Nevertheless, he was called by God. We read in the book of I Kings 19 that Elijah sat under the tree and wanted to die. Why? How could a man that was chosen by God and anointed by God find himself in a place where fear just dominated his life. Because in I Kings 18:46, he had lost all his physical strength and energy because he had ran nearly twenty miles to Jezreel—the enemy called Jezebel was looking for him to kill him. One-woman words caused him to be intimidated, fearful, and he lost his confidence, self-esteem, and made him doubtful.

Words are seeds! You see we know that God's word works as a two-edged sword, but God's word also is considered to be a seed. You see God's word is also alive just like a seed. The word of God states in John 6:63 NKJ "It is the Spirit who gives life; the flesh profits nothing. The word that I speak to you are spirit, and they are life." When God speaks it causes things to come alive as we clearly see in God's word in [12]Genesis 1:3 said, " And God said, let there be light: and there was light," and it happened. God spoke the whole world into existence through words. So, the enemy knows that words are very powerful, words are so powerful that it has caused divorces, world wars, catastrophe, and it causes men to be promoted and demoted, it brings fear, intimidation and it also brings joy and peace. This is what was happening with the prophet Elijah, the enemy was using words to antagonize and intimidated him. Anytime the enemy realizes that you are a threat to his kingdom and you have a calling on your life, he tries to use words to intimidate you from fulfilling your purpose. The enemy will use anyone to try to get his lies to you and the sad truth is he has so many volunteers that make themselves available to be used by him. The number is endless, that is why it is so important to know God's voice. Know when the Lord is speaking from the when the devil is speaking. The enemy loves to get us when we are tired, mentally, physically, and especially when were spiritually drained. You see, words are seeds and the enemy uses people to use their words to try to conquer us as Jezebel did to Elijah.

The word of God speaks about this powerful story about Elijah. In 1 Kings 17:1-7 the Bible tells us that Elijah went to the brook of Cherith as directed by God. He was to drink the brook water and eat bread and meat that the ravens would bring him there. Elijah needed to hide, far away from King Ahab and his Queen Jezebel. Ahab and Jezebel were the most wicked and evil rulers Israel had ever known. They employed 850 prophets of Baal and his consort, Ashera, and were killing the prophets of God. After Elijah told Ahab there would be no rain for years to come and not until he said so, they were determined to kill him. When Ahab married Jezebel, he created an unholy alliance with the King of Sidon, Jezebel's father. Her country worshiped Baal which was supposed to be a dominant god that controlled storms and rain. Baal and Ashera, his companion, were fertility gods. Elijah was chosen by God to defeat all of them. So regardless of how the enemy tried to intimidate or put fear in Elijah, he knew that he had a mission to fulfill. Just know that God is your deliverer.

It wasn't until Elijah heard that Jezebel wanted to kill him that the seed of fear was planted. Those negative words had Elijah running for his life, this strong man of faith allowed the word of the enemy to intimidate. For some of us, it's our past that has been chasing us, and for others, it is the voice of doubt that has been chasing us. Fear has been running after us, and if the truth be told, the things we fear not only have ran after some of us, but that fear have also caught up with us and we've been trapped in its lies. But

Jesus wants to set us free. Elijah was tired and exhausted, and then he got some bad news. Isn't that the way life is?

I am sure that Elijah wasn't the only man in the Old Testament that was depressed, but we are going to focus on Elijah as an example. This man of God experienced difficulty like most of us do, the challenges of having extremely high and low moments, and these intense fluctuations caused Elijah to suffer from the tormenting spirit of depression. This spirit of depression was out to destroy him, but the Lord always knows when to show up. The solitary moments in Elijah's life are to teach us that you can be called by God and suffer from the spirit of depression and isolation. This is not for us to harbor the spirit of depression, but we must learn how to cast it out through the word of God. I thank God that we have hope in King Jesus for deliverance from every sort of bondage.

When God applies pressure, I believe that the Lord gets the best out of His chosen vessels which are the people who have given their lives to Jesus Christ. You see, like most of us who are called by God, the prophet Elijah was sent to stop the plans of the enemy. Your past, circumstance or position doesn't determine your power; it's what you're carrying that determines your strength. It is only the anointing of God that can destroy the works of the enemy. The word of God says in [13]1 John 4:4 "Ye are of God, little children, and have overcome them: because greater is he that is in you, than he that is in the world." Never forget that the devil knows that in the end we win! The devil is sometimes referred to as an 'adversary' and when I did a little research on the word adversary, I found out that it means "an enemy or someone who opposes someone else. [14]Adversary is related to the word adverse, meaning "against or contrary" —so think of an adversary as someone whom you are fighting against." Unfortunately, there will always be a fight but have no fear, God will protect us and keep us

It's Time to Take off the Mask
Have you ever been with a group of friends and glanced over to see either a couple or another group laughing their socks off? You might think, "Hmm, those people seem to be having a good time. They are having fun." You might also say to yourself, "I wish that I was the one over there having a good time. " You might also have said to yourself that you wish that you had a particular career or were born into a certain family. Maybe you wish you could get your kids to be well-behaved like the Joneses'. I can recall when I was thirteen years old and my parents were going through a divorce, I wished I belonged to another family because my house was not a place of peace—it was a place of pain and sadness and it was Hell on earth. I don't believe our parents realized the impact the divorce had on us as children.

Well, I've come to realize that in life what you see is not always what you get. There are a lot of people out there just living a facade. We hear that word "facade" a lot and the Merriam-Webster dictionary states façade is [15]"a false, superficial, or artificial appearance or effect." I was living a facade, I was living a lie, and I wasn't happy, although I wanted people to believe that I was happy. Half of the things we do is to impress people who don't even care about us, or what we have. Christ being in our hearts and in our lives gives us an opportunity to be free from the façade.

I lacked hope, peace, and joy until I found Jesus and He rescued my soul from the pit of hell. All of our souls need rescuing, from sin and only God can do this for us. The word of God says in [16]Ephesians 3:20 "Now unto him that is able to do exceedingly and above what we can ask or think according to the power that worketh in us". What God did for me He can do it for you if you surrender and call upon His name. The word of God says in Acts 2:21, "And it shall come to pass, that whosoever shall call on the name of the Lord shall be saved." Giving my life to God was the best decision that I made in my life.

The Mask of No Self-Worth
The next spirit that was attacking me early in life was the spirit low-self-esteem, lack of self-worth, which I believe were seeds planted by the devil when my father left us. I felt rejected, unwanted, and unloved. This created a void inside my heart and doubt about what true love was meant to be. I was completely discombobulated and depressed for the next couple of years and that lasted till I started a relationship with Christ in my early twenties.

I could recall the first time that I experienced this feeling of lack of self-worth was when I realized that my father wasn't returning back home. You see, my parents always fought, and I thought that this was normal in every family. Could you imagine when dysfunctional behaviors seem like the norm because that is all I knew. So, in my mind, I thought, "Well, they've fought before and he has left for a few days and came back home," but this time, my mom was very quiet and didn't say much. But, one week turned into a few months and a few months became years. Yes, I had some serious abandonment and daddy issues.

One day out of the blue, he came over and I was so excited and happy. He sat down in the living room, and I could tell in his face that he was just as sad as me, and he just kept hugging me. The last thing that he said was, "I'm going to pick you guys up soon to take you shopping like we use to do," and I said "Okay, Daddy. I can't wait to see you." Once again, the weeks turned into months, and then I stopped hoping. I believe that once our hope is lost depression is able to find a place in our lives.

My dad was my world. He was everything to me and then he was gone. I was heartbroken and went through a season of deep depression. I started having illicit relationships and got involved with crowds of people that were partying and doing drugs. Half of the relationships that I was in at the time were so bad, detrimental, and destructive to me, emotionally and psychologically, I continued to spiral until I surrendered my heart and my life to God. I wasn't supposed to be alive, but God had a better plan for my life. Destiny wouldn't allow me to die.

This lack of self-worth was driven by the spirit of rejection, and abandonment. I felt alone and confused and felt like someone died in my life when my father left. My life was renewed and restored when I gave my heart to God. God is the father to the fatherless as is written in His word [17]Psalm 68:5 "A father of the fatherless, and a judge of the widows, is God in his holy habitation." Even though my earthly father abandoned me, but God has always been with me. Jesus is able to heal us from the pain of an absent father. Jesus became my ultimate and faithful loving father. Through the help of the Holy Spirit, I was able to forgive my father and be delivered from the spirit of rejection and abondment.

I learned that the main thing that the enemy was using was my ignorance of who I was in Christ. I didn't know my identity, nor my father. We are not defined by who the world say that we are, but we are defined by who Christ say's that we are. It is so imperative to know who we are and also teach it to our children who they are. I had to learn through the world of God that I am a child of God and I am His beloved. God loves you. So simple but not having this revelation kept me bound and trapped by the lies of the devil. Knowing who you are in Christ Jesus will save you heartache, grief and turmoil. The word of God tells me that I am a child of God:

Genesis 1:27 "So God created man in his own image, in the image of God created he him; male and female created he them."

Galatians 3:26 "For you are all children of God through faith in Christ Jesus."

Galatians 4:7 "So you are no longer a slave, but God's child; and since you are his child, God has made you also an heir."

Galatians 2:20 "I have been crucified with Christ and I no longer live, but Christ lives in me. The life I now live in the body, I live by faith in the Son of God, who loved me and gave himself for me."

John 15:11 "I have told you this so that my joy may be in you and that your joy may be complete."

Ephesians 2:4-5 "But because of his great love for us, God, who is rich in mercy, made us alive with Christ even when we were dead in transgressions–it is by grace you have been saved."

Isaiah 43:4 "Because you are precious in my eyes, and honored, and I love you, I give men in return for you, peoples in exchange for your life."

The next spirit that I wrestled with was the spirit of comparison, which the rooted by pride. Pride is a secret assassinator; it makes us feel that we are indispensable. It also makes us feel the need to have things better than others, and it makes us feel or think that we have to be on top. Pride is what kicked the devil out of heaven. Pride is deadly, even more deadly than poison, and could shorten your life and kill your God-given destiny. The word of God says in Proverb 16:18 "Pride goeth before destruction, and a haughty spirit before a fall." Trust me destruction is never too far where pride is. You must pray and keep this spirit far from your heart at all times. It will try to get the very best of us, none of us are excused from this spirit of pride attacking the believers.

Pride makes us miss our mark, destination and makes us self-reliant, self-sufficient, and makes us no longer give credit to our creator, who is God. It causes man to stop seeking the face of God for direction and instruction. Pride causes us to start living a facade and wearing masks to conform to societal norms. This need to conform has been fostered by the way society or other people view who we are. The word of God says in James 4:6 "But he giveth more grace. Wherefore he saith, God resisteth the proud, but giveth grace unto the humble." You see when you acknowledge that God is the ruler of your life and you are absolutely nothing without Him, it will keep you humble.

We weren't created by God to be ordinary nor to conform. Romans 12:2 says, "And be not conformed to this world: but be ye transformed by the renewing of your mind, that ye may prove what is that good, and acceptable, and perfect, will of God." Your healing will start when you change the way you think about things and life. You have to ask God to give you a heart like Him!

First Thing's First: Lay Down and Be Quiet

Often, it is just not one thing that goes wrong. If that was the case, we could just put all our attention to that one situation. Most of the time, when we feel that way, we have at least five problems that we are juggling all at the same time. I had to learn about self-care. Most of the time, it's not the dishes in the sink or the garbage being taken out. The real issue is the attacks that you've been getting in your mind, the affliction in your body, or the fear that has you all discombobulated.

For example, I've gone through some serious seasons of loss and physical pain, where I couldn't sleep at night. I was suffering from the spirit of insomnia due to the medications that my doctor had prescribed to me and grief. Although I was laying down, my mind was still moving like the speed of lightning. Thoughts were just going back and forth. If it happened just one or two nights or maybe a week, that wouldn't be too bad, but this went on from one day to one week, then it went from days to months. I would spend countless nights with my eyes wide open till four o'clock in the morning for several days which started to affect me physically and emotionally. I was suffering from insomnia which caused me to be irritated and cranky most of the time. In that season, I was facing several challenges and suffering from emotional trauma and grief. I felt like I was always trying to play catch-up, and I couldn't catch up.

I reminded myself in that season about King David in the Bible. He had several challenges in his life, but he was a skillful worshipper. The word of the Lord said that David was "a man after His own heart." You see, this story is about King Saul and the shepherd boy named David. Saul was the people's choice and not God's choice. King Saul was disobedient and messed up and God brought David, who came from the tribe of Judah, which meant "praise." But, if you look at David's life, it was filled with a life of challenges, struggles, battles, contradictions, internal conflict, and enemies. Yet, he always praised God in every situation. God said he found David. God is looking for a faithful worshipper, that will honor and praise Him, no matter what life is bringing them. God was able to testify that David was after His heart. God knew that although King David had failures and issues, but He also knew that David loved Him, and he wouldn't deny God His honor and praise. As a king, David had authority, riches, servants, wealth, and with all he had, he knew that in his core, at the center of it all, was God. David always remembered that when he was a shepherd boy that it was God that elevated him and granted him favor, and not man.

We need to acknowledge that all we are all we could ever be because of the love of God and His grace and mercy. The word of God says in I Corinthians 15:10 "But by the grace of God I am what I am: and his grace which was bestowed upon me was not in vain; but I labored more abundantly than they all: yet not I, but the grace of God which was with me." This is why it is so important to be grateful to God for everything that God has blessed us with. The word of God also declares God is the Alpha and Omega, which simply means that He is the beginning and the end of all things. Sometimes, you may feel emotionally bankrupt, in a financial drought, confused, and you may feel like you are losing your mind, your joy, and you're scared, but give God the praise. God is faithful to deliver you. Daily, through the Holy Spirit by faith, I wake up and declare that I am becoming the best version of myself through the guidance of the Holy Spirit. Your praise is a weapon that can bring breakthrough, healing, and deliverance, and I challenge you today to use that weapon.

You see, David always inquired of the Lord because he was humble and knew that within himself, he was insufficient, lacking, and incapable of being anything without God. We always have to remember that we are absolutely nothing without God. I always say in my prayers, "Lord, help me to completely surrender my flesh, my desires, and my needs to your will. Lord, help me to be transformed mentally and emotionally." I feel that Jesus has been my rock from day one, and He could handle all our ups and downs.

The enemy always tries to attack us when we are physically, emotionally and mentally drained; the enemy uses this as an opportunity to attack us. It is important to guard our minds during this time. Your mind is truly a battlefield. The two scriptures that I go to when I am having spiritual warfare in my mind are the following: 2 Corinthians 10:5 (KJV) "Casting down imaginations, and every high thing that exalted itself against the knowledge of God and bringing into captivity every thought to the obedience of Christ;" and Ephesians 6:17 (KJV) "And take the helmet of salvation, and the sword of the Spirit, which is the word of God." It's all about protecting your mental state through the Holy Spirit.

Through this journey called life, we will face many challenges that will make us feel as if we can't catch up, we are going through life on a treadmill, and we are getting nowhere. Yeah, I know that you have the power of God in you, but the thing that sometimes our bodies and minds need is simply to rest and be still. Sometimes you need to tell people, "Although this is important to you and you feel as if this discussion needs to happen now, I need to hit my internal reset or reboot button before I can participate." We are not Superman or Superwoman— they were just characters that someone wrote for a storyline. But we have superpower through the Holy Spirit

Be Careful with the Things You Give Your Attention to: Listen to the Voice of God

We must be very careful with the things that we give our attention to when we are going through spiritual warfare. We see this from the beginning of time, that the enemy caused Eve to get distracted and deceived by his lies. The enemy is always sending thoughts, people and things to try to get us to lose focus on our assignment, but we must be intentional with the vision that God has given us and stop focusing on the assignments that God never gave us, to people that do not care about us, people that do not have our best interest, or careers that are not in the will of God nor give us joy, or our own desires. This reminds me of Nehemiah in the Bible, he had a job in the palace serving the king, but God had given him the burden to go back and rebuild the walls.

During the time that he was rebuilding, his enemy mocked him, tried to deceive him and try to distract him from his mission but Nehemiah was determined, so determined that he built back the wall in fifty-two days. What is that thing or that assignment that God gave you that you should be focused on instead of the distractors that the enemy has put in your life. Sometimes it's good to just reflect and take inventory and start to get rid of those things in our lives that prevent us from fulfilling our divine destiny.

What we listen to enters into our ear gate. When the children of Israel were given a promise by God that they would possess the Canaanite territory, they had the promise, but they had to do the work. The Bible tells us in [18]James 2:17-20 "Even so faith, if it hath not works, is dead, being alone. Yea, a man may say, thou hast faith, and I have works shew me thy faith without thy works, and I will shew thee my faith by my works. Thou believest that there is one God; thou doest well: the devils also believe, and tremble. But wilt thou know, O vain man, that faith without works is dead?" So, the children of Israel had to make a move based on the promise, and that is exactly what it means to have faith in God. Most of the time you're not given a manual or even know what will happen next, but you just have to trust God and step out on faith and the promise that God gave you.

The enemy is cunning and also knows how to craft his lies to look like the truth. This is why it is important to know the voice of God. The Bible says in Romans 10:14: "So then faith cometh by hearing, and by hearing the word of God." When you read the word of God it builds up our faith and strengthen our relationship with God. The enemy also tries to use the time when our health is weak to attack us—the enemy is an opportunist. This is why it is vital to take care of our physical bodies. You have to realize that God has given us this one body and the word of God. It is called His temple, so we must take care of it. God is going to use our hands, our feet, and our mouth to do His will. For example, Elijah had a wonderful mountain top experience with God; he got the victory in [19]I Kings 18:16–39. I am sure that he was happy and overjoyed when God showed up and gave him victory. Then all of a sudden, fear came in because he heard that Jezebel had killed many prophets, and he was on her hit list. Depression started to seep in.

Have you ever had a wonderful thing happen in your life and then, all of a sudden, you don't know why, but the spirit of fear and depression start to try to attach itself to you? I can relate to this because I was suffering from this spirit of depression. I didn't recognize it at first. Depression often comes in our lives when we least expect it. We have to constantly meditate on the word of God and live in His presence. The enemy tries to use our mind as a target for the lies that he would like to plant. Here are some scriptures that helped me overcome the spirit of depression and the battlefield that was in my mind:

Psalm 46:10 Be still and know that I am God: I will be exalted among the heathen I will be exalted in the earth.

II Corinthians 10:4: For the weapons of our warfare are not carnal, but mighty through God to the pulling down of strongholds.

Ephesians 3:20: Now unto him that is able to do exceeding, abundantly above all that we ask or think, according to the power that worketh in us.

The Renewed Mind

Our minds are so important and the way we use our minds is very important. "The mind" (i.e., the mental faculties, reason, or understanding), is in itself, neutral. The word of God says in Philippians 2:5 "Let this mind be in you, which was also in Christ Jesus:" You have to have the mind of Christ in you. My Pastor always taught us in our Bible studies that our mind is the only part of us that could be one place and travel to another country or to our past. I read this quote by Tamara Kulish who said, [20]"Some of the heaviest burdens that we carry are the thoughts that we carry in our heads every day." Burdens weighs us down and only God is able to deliver us through His word. When you cry out to God in sincerity, He will always hear and answer your call.

Although the mind is neutral, negative thoughts diminish our faith and hope, which all comes from the enemy. We have to be sensitive to the thoughts that we are harboring in our minds. The thoughts that we feed upon will grow, so if we want to have a healthy mind, we have to fill it with the word of God and good and positive thoughts. The word of God states, Philippians 4:8: "Finally, brethren, whatsoever things are true, whatsoever things are honest, whatsoever things are just, whatsoever things are pure, whatsoever things are lovely, whatsoever things are of good report; if there be any virtue, and if there be any praise, think on these things." The best ways to keep your mind and thoughts pure is through the word of God. I especially love the scripture in Proverbs 18:21 that states, "Death and life are in the power of the tongue: and they that love it shall eat the fruit thereof." The power is not necessarily in what people say about you, but I find my hardest challenges have been with the negative things that I have said about myself. We tend to allow the situations that we face to define who we are when really; we are who God say's we are. I thank God for the word of God that has enabled my mind to be transformed through the blood of Jesus Christ.

The "renewed mind," or the mind acting under the influence of the Spirit, is very similar to how the word "conscience" is used by Bishop Butler, a preacher from England who was an influential writer and philosopher in his time. A mind that is renewed is dependent on God for everything. You have to completely surrender your will, your thoughts, and your ideology unto the Lord for God to completely use you. It is a mind that seeks and waits on the Holy Spirit for guidance and instruction, a mind that seeks truth from the word of God.

There are so many self-help books that are on the bookshelves, on YouTube, or being ordered on Amazon Prime. But if we are honest with ourselves, no matter how much self-improvement we make, or how many different skin- creams we try, or how many weight loss potions or programs we have, we, in our strength, are very limited, and without the Holy Spirit breathing in us, our minds have very narrow bounds. Says Alexander Maclaren, another theologian, "Any man that has ever tried to cure himself of the most trivial habit which he desires to get rid of, or to alter in the slightest degree the set of some strong taste or current of his being, knows how little he can do, even by the most determined effort." [21]

If you really desire a long-lasting change in your character and in your life, you must possess a deep conviction in your mind of His redemptive power. Jesus has become real to you and the Gospel of Jesus Christ has to become real in your heart and in your mind. You have to be convinced in your mind without a shadow of a doubt that Jesus Christ walked on this earth for thirty-three years, died for us, and has poured out His love and the gift of His divine Spirit upon us. Jesus' will and desire are for us to be like Him and to have eternal life. This famous theologian Alexander Maclaren stated, [22]"It is not so much what you say you believe that shapes your character; it is the little that you habitually realize. Truth professed has no transforming power; truth received and fed upon can revolutionize a man's whole character." Alexander Maclaren, in his *Expositions of Holy Scripture: Romans and Corinthians* says, [23] "We can't change our minds till we are able to believe and receive the truth that is in the word of God." The word of God brings truth to man in the most elementary way. Jesus gospel was so simple so that even a child can accept Him into their hearts. It's simple, say yes in your heart and believe and let God do the rest.

God has already created us to be great and He knew that we would hit some bumps along the way, but His grace is always there to pick us up even when all hope is lost. God has opened my eyes to see myself and how I was living a facade. So many people laugh but are actually trying to hide their pains or sorrows. Many who are wearing a facade are crying inside and going through emotional crises.

I can testify about this because I also went through a season of discouragement, depression, and despondency. I can recall when my youngest sister graduating from law school in May and passing away that summer, this took my family through a whirlwind. I felt like everything that could have been shaken within me was shaken. I was shaken, emotionally, mentally, and spiritually I was in a very dark and sad season in my life. One of the scriptures that kept my mind was Philippians 2:5: "Let this mind be in you, which was also in Christ Jesus." When we stay connected to God through reading His word and having a prayerful life, Satan doesn't have any other choice but to lose His grip. I thank God that the Lord has delivered me from depression, anxiety, and fear. Now I've got my joy back and I believe God can do that for you too!

Happiness vs. Joy

We tend to measure people's happiness and joy based on what we see on the surface, but for us to experience true joy, it must come from having Jesus Christ in our hearts. C.S. Lewis said, "Joy is the serious business of heaven."[24] It is God's desire for us to have joy and not necessarily happiness. You see, happiness is a temporary state of mind. Something needs to happen for us to be happy, but God's joy is a supernatural treasure that no matter what you are going through or facing in life, no matter what you have or don't have, you feel a sense of peace and you know that you are fulfilled in Him. You see I tried to find my joy in everything else but God and at the end of it all I was still miserable, still depressed and still felt hopeless, it wasn't until I surrendered my heart to Jesus, I experienced real joy.

No matter what you are chasing after, or what you are trying to achieve for your-self or your family, you could never be fulfilled unless you are in God. Colossians 2:10 states, "And ye are complete in him, which is the head of all principality and power:" When you have God you are free from people's opinions and judgements. When you experience real joy, you could face any storm. We are whole through the blood of Jesus Christ because Jesus Christ is our everlasting joy.

My Story of My Darkness

You may be wondering "When am I going to come out of this slump, this depression?" Some of you may be saying to yourself, "How long will I be depressed and wrestle with all these internal conflicts and addictions?" You may also be saying, "Why should I take off this mask? It has been my comfort, shelter, and hiding place for such a long time."

You see, masks can be used for two things: to cover up or hide something, and to prevent others from coming in. My laughter was my mask. When I was much younger, I used to think that laughter was an indicator of joy and happiness—until I started to understand that this was a lie, because it was my lie that I was living! It was the lie that I told myself. Yes, this was the lie that I was living in.

I made sure that I wore this mask every day so I could hide my battles, wounds, and demons. I would laugh or smile to hide the pain and mask the deep wounds of shame, rejection, and sadness that were within my soul that I carried as young as eight years of age. I thought that all I needed to do was to work on the outside and make sure that no one knew how broken I truly was on the inside. I used laughter as a defense mechanism. On the outside, I hid my pain and made sure that everyone thought that I was happy. God knows that all it was just a *big fat lie*. The truth is that I was slowly dying. Shame, coupled with a few other demons such as thoughts of rejection, failure, fear, low self-esteem, insecurity, perversion, and daddy abandonment issues had grown, festered, and had taken refuge in my heart and soul.

Sometimes, we get so mentally and emotionally comfortable in a bad situation, environment, or condition, we don't try to escape from it. I felt stuck and trapped in depression and even listened to the lies of the devil when he would say that I needed to keep the mask on. I started thinking, "Why should I remove my mask? It's not as if there's anyone that I could trust, and such a person will still love me after they know the *real* me? Who could I trust to take off my mask?" These were all lies that the devil was whispering to me and what I told myself when I was surrounded by darkness.

The combination of the weight of my sins and shame, coupled with my battle with the spirits of depression, anxiety, rejection, and low self-esteem led to a vicious cycle. I didn't know that that cycle was demonic and devilish. I didn't know how to break the cycle because I was ignorant of spiritual warfare. I was numb to my condition, to my environment, to my situation—one of the worst stages to be in. I had absolutely no feelings or emotions left that were solid or with substance and I just accepted being hopeless because I didn't know Jesus. Due to the sins that I had committed and from the abuse that I experienced as a child, I thought that I would never be free from the heavy weight of guilt and shame that I carried every day. I had no self-worth, and I was being deceived by the devil.

God can handle all your skeletons. We all have a place inside that no one knows. I don't care how close two people may be. Even if they sleep in the same bed every night and talk every day; they don't know and share *everything* about each other. Only God knows *all* the matters of the heart. God can handle your messy mess-ups, your lack, your insecurities, and your fears. You may also be saying to yourself as I did, "Do I even know how to live without it? Because the mask has become part of me." I had convinced myself to continue to hide behind it. My mask was my place of safety and comfort away from the lies that I was being tormented with.

God will make you deal with the real you, not the fake you or the one that you've worked so hard to make sure that it looks good for others. So, I was bringing that fake spirit into my time with God; I didn't feel the need to tell Him the bad things, just the good ones. In my prayer life, I was avoiding the real things that I needed deliverance from, until one day it was like the Holy Spirit said to me "I know all of you Cassandra. Every part of you I know. Nothing is hidden. I love you and I have called you."

When God spoke to me, I felt like the ton of bricks that was on my heart had been instantly removed; the weight of my shame was lifted. That very day, transformation started to take place in my life. I started to feel the presence of God and how truly it was meant to feel. I felt no shame nor embarrassment, but I felt free to be myself and speak what was truly going on in my heart and my mind. I thank God for the overflow of His presence, which heals our past and present and prepares us for our future. The Bible states in II Corinthians 3:17, "Now the Lord is that Spirit, and where the Spirit of the Lord is, there is liberty." Where is that place where you go to hide your shame, regrets, and those many things that make you uncomfortable? The time to give it to Jesus is now.

The Power of God's Divine Timing

There is nothing like God's divine timing. It was over twenty years ago when God declared that it was time for me to take off my mask. At the time, I had no idea that my life was about to change from being broken, damaged, and distressed to being free and delivered. I didn't know, but I was about to collide with my destiny. It was like God was aligning and orchestrating my steps for a divine appointment.

When the weeds of sin start to grow in our hearts, only the Holy Spirit can supernaturally remove them with His precious blood. You don't have to stay in that state of mind, and you don't have to fight these psychological battles on your own. One of my favorite songs was written by [25]Robert Lowry, a well-known 1876 hymn writer, a Baptist Minister, and professor at Lewisburg (Bucknell) University. The song says, "What can wash away our sins? Nothing but the blood of Jesus." Some people may think this is old-school, but it is as true today (and it will always be my song): nothing but the blood of Jesus Christ could have washed my sins and rescued me out of that horrible pit of depression. I learned that there is power in the blood of Jesus and He died on the cross so we can be free from every form of bondage.

The word of God says in John 10:10, "The thief cometh not, but to steal, and to kill, and to destroy: I have come that they might have life and that they might have it more abundantly." The whole purpose of God sending His son Jesus Christ to die for us is to give us the opportunity to have the abundance of His grace and mercy. God has a way of coming into our lives and removing all the negativity and rubbish that are keeping us from achieving our destiny.

It took many years of praying and fasting, submitting to the will of God, and the deliverance process for those chains to be broken off my life. I also thank God for my Pastor, Rev. Dr. Jacqueline Waite, who through the power of the Holy Spirit, was able to detect these demons that I was carrying and broke the strongholds off my life. I thank God every day for my deliverance and salvation. The devil cannot have you because you belong to Jesus. You see, the Bible says in

Romans 8:35-39:
Who shall separate us from the love of Christ? Shall tribulation, distress, persecution, famine, nakedness, peril, or sword? As it is written, for thy sake we are killed all the day long; we are accounted as sheep for the slaughter. Nay, in all these things we are more

than conquerors through him that loves us. For I am persuaded, that neither death, nor life, nor angels, nor principalities, nor powers, nor things present, nor things to come, nor height, nor depth, nor any other creature, shall be able to separate us from the love of God, which is in Christ Jesus our Lord.

Nothing You Can Do Can Keep God from Loving You
The Bible states in Hebrews 12:1, "Wherefore seeing we also are compassed about with so great a cloud of witnesses, let us lay aside every weight, and the sin which doth so easily beset us, and let us run with patience the race that is set before us." Sin is heavy and tiresome. It wears you out. Most of the time I felt like the whole world was on my shoulders and it was because I was in sin. It always felt like I was going around in circles, on this treadmill heading nowhere. I had no vision, no direction, and definitely no purpose.

The thing is that when you're about to collide with divine destiny, all bets are off because God takes full control of your deliverance. God saw me drowning, and He came in the nick of time and rescued me. I needed to yield and allow the Holy Spirit to come into my heart for me to realize that I could no longer run from my demons. Drinking and smoking could no longer satisfy nor pacify the weight of sin in my life. I couldn't escape the tormenting spirit of anxiety and depression, and I was forced to face my demons. I was coming to the end of such a dark place in my life, and God was about to give me a new chapter, another chance called GRACE!

You reach a point where you can no longer continue to live a double life, happy in front of everyone, and going home, feeling hopeless and empty. In your strength or capacity, you cannot fix yourself; you cannot break these strongholds. After a while you get tired of faking it and you realize that your freedom from sin is more important than anything else in life. You need the power of God to manifest in your life. Take it from me, that God is so in-love with you and there is absolutely nothing you can do about it. His love is infinite, and so tender and can comfort you at your very lowest point.

When God Takes Over

Once the Holy Spirit takes over, you no longer need a mask, and everyone can truly see the *real* you. I know people living today and say that they are Christians and still living with their masks. For example, there is the mask of pride, the mask of unforgiveness, and the mask of jealousy, to name a few, but God wants to deliver you and completely remove every mask. The thing I love about God is that He knows that we are hopeless without Him. He needs to strip us of everything that has kept us bound and in hiding. Do you desire to come out of hiding and truly experience joy in your life? Well, you have to let Jesus in. Not into the superficial area, but in the deeply wounded area in your heart—the area that you don't let anyone in and that dark area that you've made sure to tuck away so far that no one (not even your closest friend or your spouse knows). You have to let God in there. It makes no sense that you try to hide it from Him because He already knows.

King David wrote in the book of Psalms 139:8, "If I ascend up into heaven, thou art there: if I make my bed in hell, behold, thou art there." It's funny we live and go through life thinking that we are the ones controlling our lives, but that is not the case. The reality is that God has always been there whether we acknowledge His presence or not. When you surrender to God in your heart, you are no longer in the driver's seat. God comes in and lets you know that He is the One running the show.

I'm wondering what mask you are wearing because I had several: the funny mask, the cool mask, the seductive mask, the happy mask. All of them were lies. I learned that with Jesus, you could be your true and authentic self. Be it good, bad, or ugly, the best part of it was that His love surpassed my imagination or expectation. I never knew of such great and unfailing love. A love that looked beyond those masks and saw all my flaws, sins, weaknesses, and my doubts—but loved me anyway.

Wow! What an amazing love and what an amazing God He is. His love is never-failing and never-ending. I needed Jesus desperately and didn't know it. I was searching and constantly feeling empty as if there was more to life than constantly living this lie. I started getting tired and weary of always pretending. I was the life of the party and always planning the next big event, the next party, the next hang out, anything to get away and escape from my shame and reality of how troublesome my life had become.

I am not ashamed to share this with you because honestly it was the love of God that set me free and I am no longer bound by those spirits of depression and oppression, and most importantly, I no longer wear a mask. I no longer suffer from shame and depression and I know that I am not the only one that has gone through this experience. I thought that my life was done and that I was destined to lose, but that was before I met Jesus. Now I know that my name is Victory! I am here to tell you that there is hope in King Jesus.

Do you have anything in your life that has brought you great pain and made you feel ashamed? Well, you are not alone. I found my hope in the Lord and if you make Him the Lord of your life, you will also experience this joy that I am talking about.

The Divine Setup

I was at that place of shame and that place of emptiness when the Savior found me. I was at my wit's end, I had nowhere else to turn, and no one to turn to. I didn't know it then, but I now know that it was all God's divine set up for my life. Yes, it was a divine set up! He had to put me in a familiar environment to give me a fresh beginning.

Everything in your life has been heavenly calibrated for your divine destiny. God always divinely synchronizes our lives and allows us to be in the right place at the right time and puts us around the right people. One of my favorite stories in the word of God is about the Lord meeting the women at the well. In John 4:4 it states, "And he must go through Samaria." If Jesus, as busy as He was, stopped to deliver one woman out of her dark state, I realized that He could also do it for us. So, at the lowest state of my life—my breaking point—God was about to turn my life around and I didn't even know it. For some of us, things have to get low before we surrender to God. Things had to get dark and low for me before God had my undivided attention.

God is very specific and strategic in setting up our lives for us to collide with destiny. The story in the book of John continues in verse 6: "Being wearied with his journey, sat thus on the well: and it was about the sixth hour." The Bible was specific to state the time. God is very specific in everything that He allows to happen in your life. This is why I say what you're going through in your life is a divine set up because, in those days, wells were everywhere. This was a necessity for practically everyone. The farmers needed them for their crops and animals; people needed to drink from wells to survive. Jesus knew the specific place and hour to meet the specific need of this specific person. Sometimes, we may feel that He is not there or far away from our reach, but this story illustrates that God is ever-present in our lives and knows exactly how to show up in times of difficulty. Just as He showed up for the Samaritan woman, He will show up for you too.

Over twenty years ago, I was invited to a Monday night prayer meeting at Missionary Gloria's house. At that time, in that season that was considered the fun place to hang out, never associated this house with church, but God had a plan. It was a bit strange to me because this particular house was the house that we usually had house parties. I wanted to see it for myself. Yes, I went there out of curiosity and didn't go for prayers, but God had another plan. In Jeremiah 29:11, God says, "'For I know the thoughts that I think toward you,' saith the Lord, 'thoughts of peace, and not of evil, to give you an expected end.'" To tell you the truth, back then, I didn't believe that God existed. I didn't believe in God because of the horrible scars of my past. I went through some traumatic events in my childhood, where the enemy blinded my mind to believe that God wasn't real.

So, getting back to that Monday night. I was getting dressed to go for this prayer meeting, and all I thought of was that this seriously was just a big fat joke. Do they think that I am coming to pray?" I would soon realize that the joke was on me; it was another divine set up from God.

You see, God will divinely put you in a path of someone that will encourage your spirit or talk to you about God. It may be in a bagel shop, hair shop, barbershop, or grocery store. The Lord knows precisely the appointed time for you, and He is always ready to meet. I walked into the room with my mask on perfectly fitted. I was full of myself, and I was upset.

I don't even know why I was so distraught and upset because nobody forced me to be there. I went there out of my own free will and that is how the devil had me so blind and bound. I was crying uncontrollably, I felt as if a heavy burden was lifted off of me. I felt free from my mask. I now believe the enemy knew that he would no longer have a hold on me because I was on the verge of my breakthrough, where the chains would be broken off of my life. I believe that the enemy knows that about you too. Now that I am no longer blind by sin, I see, in retrospect, that I had to be there. Everything in Heaven and Earth had lined up my life for this moment. I had a divine appointment with my destiny. At that time, I wasn't experiencing any joy in my life. I was just going through the motions wearing my different masks. I was an absolute mess; I didn't have any hope or expectation for something better than the rut that I was in, and I didn't know that my life was about to change. This was one of the most defining moments of my life. This can be a defining moment for you also; all you have to do is say yes to God and to His will.

Are you faced with challenges in life, like a loss of a job, a sick loved one, a wayward child, or feeling like you are at the end of your rope? I want to reassure you that God is able. The Bible says in the book of Ephesians 3:20, "Now unto Him that is able to do exceedingly, abundantly above what we could ask for according to the power that worketh in us." I believe that some of you are feeling just like I felt, but trust me, Jesus was what I needed and what I was looking for all my life. He rescued me and poured His love on me. John 15:13 says, "Greater love hath no man than this, that a man lay down his life for his friends."

Some of you have been praying to God for some things and it hasn't happened yet. Remember God's delay doesn't mean denial. The Bible spoke about a certain man named Lazarus that was in John chapter 11. He was Jesus' friend, but Jesus delayed His arrival for a greater purpose. Lazarus was dead for four days. This situation seemed obscure, bleak, and close to impossible to change, but Jesus told Lazarus' sister, Martha, in John 11:25. "I am the resurrection, and the life: he that believeth in me, though he were dead, yet shall he live." Her faith had been shaken and she had lost all hope.

Often, the Lord will let the situation get a bit stinky before He shows up, but one thing that you can count on is that He will always show up in glory. All you have to do is believe, even when it looks and seems impossible. I was walking around dressed-up, but I was spiritually dead, and nobody knew it. Yes, dead in my hope, in my joy, and most importantly in my spirit. Not even the closest people to me could help me, but God came and rescued me. Romans 10:9 says, "That if thou shalt confess with thy mouth the Lord Jesus, and shalt believe in thine heart that God hath raised him from the dead, thou shalt be saved."

As you are reading this book, I pray that if you haven't already accepted Jesus into your heart that the Holy Spirit will come into your heart and break down all the silos and walls that the enemy has created in your heart and allow Jesus into your heart. Jesus will not only resurrect you out of your dead situation, but He also can give you a new start. Today, I declare a new beginning over your life. You see, Jesus came and died on the cross so that you can have joy. You have every right to have peace and joy; don't allow the enemy to tell you anything different.

Searching the Hearts and Setting Us Free
Even after I got saved and had given my life to Christ, I continued to carry a lot of shame and guilt for such a long time. The shame was so overwhelming, it was tormenting me and affecting my prayer life. I wasn't honest in my prayer life. I would wake up in a cold sweat. I didn't know that I was in spiritual warfare. I was avoiding the real issues I needed deliverance from until one day, it was like the Holy Spirit said to me, "I know all of you, Cassandra, every part of you, and I still love you."

Because we are limited as humans to our five senses and we are outside the spiritual realm of God, we tend to look on the outside to figure out what is going on with people on the inside. What I love about the God I serve is that He knows how to get to our core, that part of us that we don't want anyone to see or to know about—the depth of our soul. The Holy Spirit does an amazing job of searching the hearts of men. The word of God speaks about the working of the Holy Spirit in the heart of men and it says the following:

> **Hebrews 4:12, KJV:** For the word of God is quick, and powerful, and sharper than any two- edged sword, piercing even to the dividing asunder of soul and spirit, and of the joints and marrow, and is a discerner of the thoughts and intents of the heart."

> **Ezekiel 36:26, ESV:** And I will give you a new heart, and a new spirit I will put within you. And I will remove the heart of stone from your flesh and give you a heart of flesh.

> **Psalms 34:18:** The Lord is near to the brokenhearted and saves the crushed spirit.

> **Jeremiah 17:9–10, ESV:** The heart is deceitful above all things, and desperately sick; who can understand it? I the Lord search the heart and test the mind, to give every man according to his ways, according to the fruit of his deeds.

What I love about the Holy Spirit is that no matter how deep you think you've buried the shame, broken-heartedness, regrets, lies, abuse, or how much you've folded and tucked that pain away, God has a way of shining a light on it and unraveling those secrets in our souls that have kept us bound. Jesus came to set us free. You may be asking what I'm referring to. I am talking about the abuse, the molestation, the rape, the shame, the lie, the secret addiction, you name it. The Holy Spirit knows how to dig deep into the soul of man and remove all our guilty stains with the word of God. The word of God says in Micah 7:19 "He will have compassion upon us; he will subdue our iniquities, and thou wilt cast all their sins into the depths of the sea." Which simply means God has forgotten them, so you need to let them go because God wants to give you a fresh new start.

The Enemy Gets Upset
I had just given my life to God, I had started to walk in the faith, and I was eager to learn about God. My Pastor started teaching me how to pray. I would go home and pray. However, I would have these bad, tormenting dreams that would grip me with fear. It would make me not want to explore deep spiritual things because I was scared to have these tormenting dreams, but all of that was a plot of the enemy to keep me from getting the gifts and the calling that God had on my life.

One night, after I had prayed during a prayer service, I dreamt that I was surrounded by demons. They pinned me on a cross that was suspended in midair, and there was absolutely nothing beneath me but pure darkness. They opened up my mouth and I was bound at my hand and feet. They pushed their hands in my mouth and they started pulling out my teeth one by one. I could feel the pain every time they pulled a tooth; I felt the pain from my head to toe. I was in so much pain that the only thing that I struggled to do while I had a chance was mustering the strength to scream out "Jesus!" and wake up out of my dream.

That was the first time that I literally saw demons. I called my leaders, frightened, and my Pastor said, "The enemy is trying to scare you and intimidate you so you would stop praying." Although I was fearful, I decided that night that I would conquer that fear and pray to God and declare myself free from bondage, and during my prayer, the Holy Spirit just gave me this boldness. From that night, I wasn't afraid anymore. The chains of fear were broken that night. The Holy Spirit gave me the courage and strength to begin to pray with authority knowing that I had God and the whole entire heaven backing me up. I proceeded and continued to pray with boldness and confidence that God was with me, and things started to shift in my prayer life. I wonder what chains are keeping you bound. When the enemy sees and realizes that you are a threat to his kingdom, he will send his imps and demons to intimidate and scare you from receiving the power of God. Today, you can pray and break every stronghold and every chain that has been keeping you bound.

The enemy wants to derail our lives by making us lose our joy. Remember the day that you no longer saw the bright sunshine? That sunshine that reminded you that you were alive.

Well, you shouldn't feel bad because I can't remember either. I can't remember the day that I stopped laughing until my belly ached, or the time that I stopped looking forward to the nice, chill air of fall, or how I stopped enjoying watching creation give praises unto God. It takes time—days, months, years—for things to begin to spiral. But all of a sudden, you realize that you are in a dark place. You ask yourself, "How in the world did I get here? How did I let my life get this bad? How did I become so discombobulated?"

Ask yourself: how far have you gotten in the hole of depression and oppression? This book will share my journey from how I lost my joy to how I got it back again from the enemy. I will offer some tools that you can use in the word of God to pull you out of the pit.

Sadness and depression are a dark place where the enemy wants to keep you. It's a lonely, dark place because you are constantly having this battle in your mind. I am not overlooking the struggle, but you can't magnify your situation more than what we know to be true. The truth is that the joy of the Lord is your strength.

List five masks that you need to remove to move forward:

1. _____
2. _____
3. _____
4. _____
5. _____

Chapter 2:
True Joy

Joy is prayer, joy is strength; joy is love; joy is the net of love by which you can catch souls. —Mother Teresa

Have you ever asked yourself this question? "Am I genuinely experiencing the joy of the Lord?" Have you ever wondered if it is possible to live in a place of joy and peace? Yes, there is a place where there is true freedom from doubt and fear and there is a place where you have liberty in God's presence. The enemy may have put thoughts in your mind that this is impossible. I say that you *can* live a life filled with joy and peace. The key is living life with Jesus Christ.

I have noticed how our society has shifted and things have changed so much. I loved the eighties. It seemed like it was summer all the time (or maybe that was just in my mind). It was fun times for me, but of course, I was a teen with neither stress nor responsibilities.

I was acting like I had joy, but I never really had joy. The world has it all wrong in the pursuit of happiness. Many people base their happiness and joy on their accomplishments, degrees, networks, and other things they have achieved in life. Others base theirs on their careers, their friends, and so on. What the world defines as joy and happiness is very superficial and has very little to do with what matters to God; it is fleeting. When people smile and laugh in your nice, luxury corporate office, or have a great time on the soccer field, does that indicate they are experiencing joy? No, oftentimes, people mask their pain and sadness through laughter. Laughter doesn't necessarily confirm the joy in a man's heart. One of my favorite Bible scholars, C. S. Lewis said, [26]"Joy is the serious business of heaven." God desires that His children have joy.

Back in the day, we would have to call or page someone in order for us to have a conversation with them on the phone. (Yes, I know I am dating myself right now. I am from the Soul Train era.) I remember how excited I was when I got my first job in a mall at Burger King. I had saved my first paycheck to buy a beeper, and I felt on top of the world. Then that feeling faded too, like everything else in life; it is all fleeting. Everything fades away and changes, but God does not. He remains the same today, tomorrow, and forever. Back in the day, you could not find out about someone unless you called them on the phone. We had to reach out to them or meet them. But now, if you want to know what someone had for lunch or where they went during the holidays, all you have to do is to go on social media.

Social media is artificial and superficial; it's not reality. People spend several hours trying to get the perfect lighting or the perfect makeup before they put up a post. It's funny because people will go and do a YouTube video to convince us that they woke up with their makeup and hair perfectly done, but this is not true. According to a report in the British Medical Journal written by David Smallwood, an addiction expert, [27]"... social networking sites are fueling insecurity and creating an unhealthy obsession with building large friend lists among certain vulnerable groups. In addition, they may also foster "an unhealthy competitive spirit about popularity; social networks may augment feelings of rejection when friend requests are denied." Another study reported by The Daily Mail says that being "addicted to social networking sites like Facebook or Myspace can be harmful to health because it triggers people to isolate themselves and that the users are being drawn into an artificial world, increasing the risk of serious negative health effects." I also saw a video that said every time you go on Pinterest or Facebook and you click on something, it lets out a chemical called dopamine, which is similar to what happens when someone is addicted to alcohol or drugs.

Can you imagine this is why young people and even adults are so addicted to it? But God has already told us who we are. The Bible states:

Psalms 139:14: I will praise thee; for I am fearfully and wonderfully made: marvelous are thy works; and that my soul should knoweth right well.

I Peter 2:9: But ye are a chosen generation, a royal priesthood, an holy nation, a peculiar people; that ye should shew forth the praises of him who hath called you out of darkness into his marvelous light.

The problem is that we are constantly looking for people to validate and define us so that we can feel that we have a sense of purpose. But our affirmation shouldn't come from people but from God. We need what is called 'God-confidence' and not 'self-confidence' because this flesh will fail us, but God is our source of strength. Today we live and choose our happiness based on our likes on Twitter, Facebook, and Instagram. We should not depend on any external factors such as social media to find our joy; real joy comes from having a relationship with God. God's word says that we are the apple of His eyes. We look at the reality shows, our schools, and our circle of friends to raise our family or to build our marriages, but if we truly want to know who we are, we have to read the word of God. We need to learn that God is our ultimate judge, and He knows the condition of our hearts, and if we are His children, we have been sealed with His blood.

Definitions of Joy

Joy doesn't come from anything external, or superficial, and it does not come from our environment, jobs, mate, children, talents, skills, titles, gifts, or the people we know. True joy comes from knowing who Jesus Christ is and the investment that He has made in us. God and only God can give men complete joy. [28]Webster's New World Dictionary defines joy as synonymous with "happy," "glad," and "cheerful." A thesaurus relates it to "exultation," "rapture," "satisfaction," and "pleasure." Merriam-Webster's dictionary specifically defines it as "a very glad feeling; happiness; great pleasure; delight." It also refers to the source or cause of delight.

These definitions only define the expression of wonderful emotion. They fail to consider the causes of joy, the circumstances in which it is expressed or its longevity. The Bible presents a much more complex virtue than these definitions indicate. Joy appears eighty-eight times in the Old Testament in twenty-two books and fifty-seven times in the New Testament. God's Holy Spirit produces joy. The words joy, joyfulness, joyfully, joyous, and [29]*chara* (which means "joy, delight" and is akin to *chairo*, "to rejoice") is found frequently in Matthew, Luke, and in John, and once in Mark. It is mentioned in James 1:2, where it is connected with falling into trials. In the book of Galatians 5:22, it is considered one of the fruits of the Spirit; actually, the second fruit.

The Greek and Hebrew definitions of the words translated as joy and its synonyms are virtually the same as their English counterparts, except for the one whose specific definition is not "joy," but "blessed." The Greek word *makarios* reveals much about some of the major sources of biblical joy. It frequently appears as the first word in the well-known Beatitudes the Sermon on the Mount as in Matthew 5:3, "Blessed are the poor in spirit, for theirs is the kingdom of heaven."

[30]Spiros Zodhiates's Complete Word Study Dictionary gives a more comprehensive definition:

> Blessed, possessing the favor of God, that state of being marked by fullness from God. It indicates the state of the believer in Christ, said of one who becomes a partaker of God's nature through faith in Christ. The believer is indwelt by the Holy Spirit because of Christ and as a result, should be fully satisfied no matter the circumstances. Makarios differs from the word "happy" in that the person is happy who has good luck (from the root *hap*, meaning luck as a favorable circumstance). To be makarios, blessed, is equivalent to having God's kingdom within one's heart. Aristotle contrasts makarios to the word *endees*, "the needy one." Makarios is one who is in the world yet independent of the world. His satisfaction comes from God and not from favorable circumstances.

Joy is also known as a state of mind and an orientation of the heart. It is a settled state of contentment, confidence, and hope. It is something or someone that provides a source of happiness.

Knowing Real Joy

I never had joy before I knew Christ. Although I appeared to be very happy as I mentioned earlier and full of life on the outside but inside, I was dying slowly. I used to feel so unfulfilled and detached from everything around me. I tried to find that sense of peace and joy, but nothing helped. The parties, the drugs, smoking, drinking, illicit relationships, and many other things I did to attempt to pacify the depression were no longer enough. I needed more because the emptiness was getting bigger and the bad habits no longer satisfied my soul, but I didn't know how to find it. I was seeking for joy in the wrong places. I didn't have happiness. I kept on trying to find ways to find happiness and joy, but they never lasted.

Real joy isn't just a smile or a laugh; it is a state of mind. You have to choose to have the joy of the Lord in your heart. Real joy is deep and everlasting; it doesn't leave quickly nor fade away. If you get upset over the small things, check yourself to see if you have joy. If you find yourself easily offended, check to see if you have real joy. A lot of people are walking around with no joy or peace, and without joy, there is no hope. The Bible says in the book of Romans 15:13 (ESV), "May the God of hope fill you with all joy and peace in believing, so that by the power of the Holy Spirit you may abound in hope." Since joy is given by God and something that He wants us to have, we need to fight for it, try to have it, and keep it! When we truly have the joy of the Lord, we'll know it and the people around us will feel it. It's not enough that we have joy, but the psalmist didn't just have joy; he had "exceeding joy." This means overflowing with joy, having joy in its fullness, and being okay with whatever life brings you: good, bad, happy, or sad.

Powerful Scriptures on Joy

Zephaniah 3:17: "The LORD thy God in the midst of thee is mighty; he will save, he will rejoice over thee with joy; he will rest in his love, he will joy over thee with singing."

Romans 12:12: Rejoicing in hope; patient in tribulation; continuing instant in prayer;

Romans 15:13: Now the God of hope fill you with all joy and peace in believing that ye may abound in hope, through the power of the Holy Ghost.

Philippians 4:4: Rejoice in the Lord always: and again I say, Rejoice.

Galatians 5:22: But the fruit of the Spirit is love, joy, peace, longsuffering, gentleness, goodness, faith,

John 16:24: Hitherto have ye asked nothing in my name: ask, and ye shall receive, that your joy may be full.

I Peter 1:8: Whom having not seen, ye love; in whom, though now ye see him not, yet believing, ye rejoice with joy unspeakable and full of glory:

Proverbs 17:22: A merry heart doeth good like a medicine: but a broken spirit drieth the bones.

James 1:2-4: My brethren, count it all joy when ye fall into divers temptations; knowing this, that the trying of your faith worketh patience. But let patience have her perfect work, that ye may be perfect and entire, wanting nothing.

John 16:22: And ye now therefore have sorrow: but I will see you again, and your heart shall rejoice, and your joy no man taketh from you.

Romans 14:17: For the kingdom of God is not meat and drink; but righteousness, and peace, and joy in the Holy Ghost.

Psalms 118:24: This is the day which the LORD hath made; we will rejoice and be glad in it.

Psalms 43:4: Then will I go unto the altar of God, unto God my exceeding joy: yea, upon the harp will I praise thee, O God my God.

Accepting the Abundant Grace of God
The grace of God is simply God's favor and kindness toward mankind. There are several blessings you can receive by having the grace of God upon your life. Grace is the love of God shown to the unlovable. That is why the Bible is filled with stories of people that society had said are "good for nothing" or sinful. But those are the ones whom Jesus spent time with and healed and delivered. The best form of grace that we've received is Jesus Christ dying on the cross. This is the gift that we received called salvation that we could never repay. Although sometimes we fail God and fall short, He still gives us His grace even when we don't deserve it. John Stott once said, [31]"Grace is love that cares and stoops and rescues."

If we know that God has sent His only begotten son to die a shameful death on Calvary so that we may have eternal life, we can, therefore, confidently boast in the cross of Jesus. God's desire is for all His children to have abundant life. We, as God's children, receive forgiveness through God's grace. You see, we deserved death, we were guilty as charged, but God said, "Yes, I know that mankind is guilty, but I am going to give them my only begotten son to come on Earth and die for them to remove those guilty charges." We had no hope, we were lost, but because of grace, we are here today. If we genuinely believed this, we wouldn't focus on who doesn't like us, who doesn't approve of us, or how many likes we have on Facebook or Instagram.

You see, every morning we wake up, we are able to take a breath, and our heart is still beating, we have hope; each morning we get new grace. I am who I am because of the grade of God. The word of God says that God "called us to a holy calling because of His own purpose and grace" (2 Timothy 2:1). God's grace gives us a fresh new start and new opportunities. It is very clear that we are loved by the only divine being that we can truly count on, which is the Almighty God. When you need strength for living, it comes from the grace of God, which is mentioned also in Hebrew 13:9: "Do not be carried away by all kinds of strange teachings. It is good for our hearts to be strengthened by grace, not by eating ceremonial foods, which is of no benefit to those who do so."

Please, I beg of you: try not to waste your precious time by focusing on your bio or your psyche. You will never find peace. It will always leave you disappointed and unfulfilled. You can't fix yourself; that is why we have to depend on God to fix and complete us. The word of God says in the book of [32]Colossians 2: 9-10, "For in Him dwelleth all the fullness of the Godhead bodily. And ye are complete in him, which is the head of all principality and power." Always remember that Christ came and died on the cross so that we may have a 'zoe' life. Zoe is a Greek word meaning life. Jesus died so we can live a life filled with joy and peace. Once we accept this abundant grace of God, we will always search for ways to feed our spirit man, by meditating on the word of God and spending time in His presence. The same word [33]"life" there means in Greek:

1. Bios, in Luke 8:14: "... anxieties and riches and pleasure of this life."

2. Zoe, in John 1:4: "In Him was life, and the life was the light of men."

Always remember that God promised us that He will be with us always. Hebrew 13:5 says, "Let your conversation be without covetousness; and be content with such things as ye have: for he hath said, I will never leave thee, nor forsake thee." In the latter part of this scripture, it tells us that God will never leave us, no matter what we are going through or what we are facing, God is with us and He is for us. God never fails and His promises are true; we can count on them. His Holy Spirit will always abide with us. Grace is a gift given to us by God. There is absolutely nothing that you can do to earn this. You can't work for it, but God gives grace to us in abundance and freely.

Meditating on the Word of the Lord
The word meditation comes from the Latin word meditārī, which has a range of meanings including to "reflect on," "to study," and "to practice." Meditating on the word is effective and important. The word of the Lord says in Psalms 1:1–3:

> Blessed is the man that walketh not in the counsel of the ungodly, nor standeth in the way of sinners, nor sitteth in the seat of the scornful. But his delight is in the law of the Lord, and in his law doth he meditates day and night. And he shall be like a tree planted by the rivers of water, that bringeth forth his fruit in his season; his leaf also shall not wither, and whatsoever he doeth shall prosper.

Meditating also helps you grow in your character and your moral values. The more you meditate, the more the Holy Spirit will show you your flaws and those things in you that need to be removed out of your life.

One of my favorite scripture is Joshua 1:8: "This book of the laws shall not depart out of thy mouth; but thou shalt meditate therein day and night, that thou mayest observe to do according to all that is written therein; for then thou shalt make thy way prosperous, and then thou shalt have good success." God spoke to Joshua after the death of his leader Moses, and I am sure that he was filled with doubt and fear, so God had to reassure him that He had chosen him. The promises of God are yes and Amen!!

You see, it's all about spending time in the word of God. The word of God says meditate day and night, so you should constantly be in His word and in His presence. Meditating on the word of God gives you direction and stability. Meditating allows you to root in God and it gives you a firm foundation. You learn about yourself and you learn who God is when you meditate on the word of God. This gives you a better understanding of the word of God. Meditation gives you clarity and allows the Holy Spirit to speak to you and gives you discernment. You see, meditating on His word gives us that anchor and the fortitude that we need when we are facing adversities. When you meditate on the word of God, it starts to take root in your heart, and it springs up in those moments when you don't know what to do and you feel discouraged. It is those same words that will help you get through tough times.

Chapter 3: I Choose Joy

> Busy is a Choice.
> Stress is a Choice.
> Joy is a Choice.
> Choose Well! —Ann Voskamp

Joy does not simply happen to us. We have to choose joy. We have to choose joy and keep choosing it every day.—Henri Nouwen

You can't wait for everything to be perfect before you decide to start to enjoy your life. There must be something that you can begin to give God thanks for, even if it's for a beautiful sunny day, or the moment you get to spend with your loved ones. I have learned to appreciate the great and small things that God does for us. Joy is always possible to attain, and really, it's a choice. It is said that our brains are constantly making decisions and making choices. For example, we make major decisions like where we are going to live and where we are going to work, and we make minor decisions such as what outfit we are going to wear, which ice cream flavor we want, and which restaurant we are going hang to out at. They're all choices that we make throughout our lives. We have been given options, which requires us to make a choice.

We have countless decisions that we are making throughout the day and sometimes we don't even realize we are making these choices. That is why marketing is so vitally important to companies. Companies invest heavily in marketing; they employ countless measures to assure that their customers choose them because they know that they are bombarded and flooded with so many options. Don't let the devil lie to you—you have options to choose from.

Joy is also a choice that you have to make. The word of God tells us in Nehemiah 8:10, "For the joy of the Lord is your strength." You must decide that you will have the joy of the Lord, no matter what. In the middle of last year, I was struggling with negative thoughts. I was experiencing intense psychological warfare. I was going through a season of depression in my life. I had several traumatic episodes that were happening at the same time. So, one day, I was talking to my Pastor about something, and she made a profound statement. "You can choose the things you want to hold on to and what you want to let go of. We all have that choice."

The light bulb went off. That was a prophetic moment in which God was speaking to me through my Pastor and that one word "choice" changed my life. Those words were exactly what my spirit needed to hear—they were so liberating. It was just that simple: the minute I said in my mind that "I am going to let it go," little by little, it left, and eventually it was gone. I had to let go of all the pain, betrayal, and grief, and I chose joy. I give all the glory to God for delivering me from the plans of the devil for my life.

Sometimes we baby negative thoughts. We pamper them and we feed them, instead of killing them. Whatever thoughts we feed will only get bigger. We need to feed the positive thoughts with the word of God. Sometimes we have to let go of the picture of what we thought life would be and trust God in the process and in the journey. Philippians 2:5 states, "Let this mind be in you, which was also in Christ Jesus:" When we do this, we learn to find joy in the present story that we are currently living.

You Can't Con God
In the Bible, there was a king named King Saul who was given a specific assignment from God through the prophet Samuel. In the book of I Samuel chapter 15, Saul was told by the prophet Samuel that he must kill all the Amalekites. But King Saul didn't rely on God; instead, he chose to do his own things and saved the king, the best sheep, oxen, lambs, and all that was good. Of course, he tried to justify his actions by saying it was the people that told him to do it, but that was a lie. Every time we try to take control of the situation or determine our own outcomes, it always leads to a disaster. That is why the word of God says in Proverbs 3:5-6 "Trust in the Lord with all thine heart; and lean not unto thine own understanding. In all thy ways acknowledge him, and he shall direct thy paths."

We must learn that God cannot be bribed, coned nor manipulated because He is in control of everything, and He knows our hearts. The word of God says that it is always better to be obedient than to present God with sacrifices. You can never go wrong when you honor God through obedience. The word of God states in Jeremiah chapter 17:9-10 "The heart is deceitful above all things, and desperately wicked: who can know it? I the Lord search the heart, I try the reins, even to give every man according to his ways, and according to the fruit of his doings." God knows our hearts.

God has proven to me time after time how much He honors our obedience. Throughout my journey, not every time that God spoke to me, I was obedient; sometimes I wasn't obedient because of my flesh. If you live according to your flesh, you will never be able to please God. The flesh never gravitates to the things of

God, but it wants to pull you out of God's presence. Sometimes I murmured, complained, shed some tears, and had to beg God to forgive me, but through prayer and the word of God, I yielded my flesh and spirit to His will, knowing that in the end, He truly knows what is best for me, and I am loved by Him. Sometimes, I was kicking and fussing on my knees, complaining, whining, and sometimes even reasoning with God, but once I started to worship and pray to God, the Lord supernaturally set a fire in my soul that burned out that part of me that wanted to do my own thing. My spirit man became the voice that won. You will win if you submit yourself to the right voice.

God Is Arranging Our Situations
What a delight it is to know that God is concerned about all of us, the very intricate, intimate details of our lives. Luke 12:7 says, "But even the very hairs of your head are all numbered. Fear not therefore: ye are of more value than many sparrows." You are valuable to God and you are precious in God's sight. God has created you in His image for His glory!

I can recall when I was attending New Greater Bethel Bible Institute in Bronx, New York, and I had just started my first real corporate job, and there was an opportunity for me to go get my MBA, but there were so many obstacles and hinderance, that I was running out of time to start school. I remember vividly praying to God and I said, "Lord, I just want your will to be done in my life and that alone, if it's your will for me to go back to school, just let me know and if not that's okay too, and I'm fine with that." I said the prayer on Saturday night and then Monday at New Greater Bethel we were having our monthly chapel service and Dr. Caswell H. Morgan, who is the Dean of New Greater Bethel Bible Institute was closing the night service and started to pray. In his prayer he started to make some declaration and I was just in agreement and then I heard him say, " there is a young lady that the Lord told me to tell you that He is going to give you a blessing, you need $10,000 for school and God said that He is going to grant it to you." I knew God was real, and I knew that I prayed but I cried the entire night, I couldn't believe it, God was so real for me that evening. I was sobbing because I was so amazed how much God was concerned to answer my prayer. The next day it was like the Lord had opened every door and I just walked through it, I got the $10,000 within two days and finished my program. When you are truly sincere to God expect him to answer, it may not be the way you think He should answer but at the end of the day, our Father knows what is best for all of his children. God has proven Himself to be faithful in my lifetime and time again. I am sure if you start reflecting on how many times that God has come through for you, it will be countless times for you too.

Stop feeding the negative thoughts that you are struggling with and begin to replace those thoughts with the promises of God. I believe that the Bible has over 365 promises, so there is one for every day of the year, so meditate on that and the miracles that He is working in your life. You know you have to figure out ways to give God thanks in your current situation. When you have learned that when you've been given sour lemons, you must learn how to make lemonade. The situation seems as if it is long, but it is very temporary in God's eyes. Also, choose your battles. Decide what you are going to spend your energy on; it doesn't make sense to worry when God already has it all figured out. The word of God says in Philippians 4:6, "Be careful for nothing; but in everything by prayer and supplication with thanksgiving, let your requests be made known unto God."

Choosing Something New

It's always hard to do something new, but you have to come out of your comfort zone in order to grow. You will never grow if you keep on doing the same thing over and over again. Change is not easy, but it is necessary for us to grow. Sometimes when God see's we are reluctant to make changes, He will put us in situations where we are forced to change, He either changes us, the people around us or the situation, but one way or another change will happen for all of us.

When I was in high school, I wanted to try out for the volleyball team. One day, I was curious to see what was going on in the gym room. I realized that there was a tryout. I was just starting to say to myself, "This is interesting." So out of nowhere, I heard the same interesting voice, and she said "Hey, are you just going to stand there or are you coming to tryouts for the team?" I was intimidated and very shy, and I had a choice to make. I could either continue to look on from the sidelines or attempt to be a part of something new.

When trying something new, it could be scary and intimidating, but new beginnings are always in the equation of God. How many things have you wanted to do in your life, but because it would mean that you have to come out of your comfort zone, you chose not to even try? How many God-opportunities you have missed because you weren't willing to come out of your comfort zone? How many times were your dreams shattered because of fear?

The volleyball coach named Mrs. Appiah, which was one of the best persons in my life at that time said that try outs would be for the entire week. I loved Mrs. Appiah because she was one of the first African American women that I saw that was fierce and strong and she believed in me. That night, I tossed and turned because I knew that I would love to try out, but it looked intimidating and I was scared: scared of failing, scared of being rejected, and scared of not making it on the team. I remembered that my mom always told me that there is nothing you shouldn't do because of fear. She told me, "Now, if you choose not to do it, that is your choice, but never let fear stop you." I was looking at her with a puzzled look and she said, "You know why? Because there is nothing that you are facing or would like to do that someone else hasn't already done. Everything that you want to do someone else has probably done it before, and if they did it, so can you." That was the little push that I needed. Later on, I learned that even the Bible tells us that in Ecclesiastes 1:9, "History merely repeats itself. It has all been done before. Nothing under the sun is truly new" (NLV). Most of the things that you are afraid of have already been conquered!

So, when I woke up, I had a decision to make. I had two choices: I could either let the fear conquer me or go to tryouts after school. I had to start speaking to myself, "What is the worst thing that could happen if I don't make it? There is life after failure. The enemy will have you locked in a prison of fear because of what if's, but you will never know unless you try." I woke up and packed an extra t-shirt.

The entire day leading up to the tryouts, I was nervous because I didn't know what to expect. During elementary school and middle school, I went to a little Catholic school in Brooklyn named Our Lady of Refuge. Everybody knew each other. When we moved to New Jersey, and I had to go to a public high school. It was a new environment, new people—everything was so scary, and it was twice as big as what I was used to. So, toward the end of the day, I started to think about the tryouts even more. I was thinking, "Am I really going to do this?" I was debating if I should do this or just go home. I don't know how, but I took my first step out to the gym. Whoever is reading this book I want you to consider that one thing that you need to step out on faith to do, that thing that you know that God has called you to do but you have allowed fear to put doubt in your heart. It's time to replace your fears and doubts and negative thoughts with FAITH!

You Have to Make a Move: Flip the Script
I am convinced that, in life, the hardest thing to do is to start, to take that very first step, to wri that very first word, to sing that very first note. You know why? There are so many voices in your mind telling you that you're a failure, you are not going to make it, you are not good enough, you can't handle it, and you are not qualified. You see, the only way the enemy can stop you is to put enough fear and intimidation in you so that you will not try. The hardest part of the battle is to make the first step. But to reach your destiny, you have to make a move.

You have to know that He is the Alpha and Omega the first and the last. He will enable you to start that business, to start that ministry, to be the good parent that you want to be, to start that course that you've always wanted to take. All you have to do is to step out with faith. You have to trust God in your darkest hour and your brightest day. You must always remember that God designed you on purpose and also for a purpose!

When your thoughts start to say the following phrases, flip the script. When I say, "flip the script," I mean you need to change how you speak and think about yourself and meditate on these suggested verses:
1. You are weak. You can't handle anything: "But the people that do know their God shall be strong and do exploits" (Daniel 11:32).
2. You are dumb, and you will never get this: "I will praise thee; for I am fearfully and wonderfully made: marvelous

are thy works; and that my soul knoweth right well." (Psalm 139:14).
3. You can't accomplish your dreams: "I can do all things through Christ which strengtheneth me" (Philippians 4:13).
4. No one loves me: "For God so loved the world, that he gave his only begotten son, that whosoever believeth in Him, should not perish, but have everlasting life. For God sent not his son into the world to condemn the world; but that the world through him might be saved" (John 3:16–17).
5. I am not good enough: "Having predestined us unto the adoption of children by Jesus Christ to himself, according to the good pleasure of his will, to the praise of the glory of his grace, wherein he hath made us accepted in the beloved" (Ephesians 1:6).
6. I am worthless; God didn't call me: "Even every one that is called by my name: for I have created him for my glory, I have formed him; yea, I have made him" (Isaiah 43:7).
7. You will always be broke: "He raises the poor from the dust and lifts the needy from the ash heap" (Psalms 113:7).
8. I am sick and will always be sick: "Who his own self bare our sins in his own body on the tree, that we, being dead to sins, should live unto righteousness: by whose stripes ye were healed" (I Peter 2:6).
9. I am ashamed of my past: "Remember ye not the former things, neither consider the things of old" (Isaiah 43:8).
10. I am not good enough: I will praise thee; for I am fearfully *and wonderfully* made: marvelous *are thy* works; and *that my* soul knoweth right well" (Psalms 139:14).
11. I am a loser: "Nay, in all these things we are more than conquerors through him that loved us" (Romans 8:37).

12. This sickness is going to be my end: When Jesus heard that, he said, this sickness is not unto death, but for the glory of God, that the son of God might be glorified thereby" (John 11:4)

Name five things you love about yourself or your personality:

1._____
2._____
3._____
4._____
5._____

Chapter 4:
Accepting God's Love

> He began to create, he began actually to redeem,
> but he never began to love.
> —Charles Spurgeon.

God loves you no matter what and there is absolutely nothing that you can do about it.

Yes, I know it's hard to fathom this thought, but there is zero—zilch—you can do to keep God from loving you. God's love never fails, and it is expressed through His son, Jesus Christ.

This was hard for me to accept. For years, I had trouble defining what true love was. I thought I knew what love was because of the way my father loved, but that was soon tainted with negative thoughts after my father left. The spirit of rejection and insecurity was planted within me. This messed up my entire perception of what love was. From the minute my father walked out the door, days passed by and I kept hoping that he would come back. I thought to myself, "Usually, when my parents have a fight, he goes to his brother's house, but he always comes back." It wasn't until a few weeks later did I realize that he was gone for good.

After my father left, I was constantly looking for someone to replace that love. It wasn't until I had an encounter with God, at the lowest point of my life, did I realize that although I had been rejected and did many things that brought me shame and disgrace, God still loved me. Yes, as messed up, insecure, and bitter as I was, He still loved me. It was when I felt the love of Jesus that I truly experienced joy in my life.

Just Come to the Love of God
I have heard this line countless times from people that I invite to attend church and it goes like this: "I have to get my life right and fix this before I come to the Lord." No, just come. You feel beat up by life, rejected, unloved, you've committed a crime, you carry shame, just come. I don't care what you've done in the past that you think disqualifies you from the love of God. That is a lie from the devil to discourage you. The word of God says in **Matthew 11:28-30**:

> 28: Come unto me, all ye that labour and are heavy laden, and I will give you rest.
> 29: Take my yoke upon you, and learn of me; for I am meek and lowly in heart: and ye shall find rest unto your souls.
> 30: For my yoke is easy, and my burden is light.

Just come to God with your broken self; just come filled with doubt and fear. Jesus will never disappoint you. He has no prerequisite to give you His love. He created you for His glory. When you don't know the love of Jesus, you can never experience real joy. God has a well of love and joy that can never run dry. God is the only one that can give us true rest.

God's love never changes and never ends. The best part about it is that Jesus doesn't base His love for us on our status, pedigree, background, level of education, talents, or skills. He just loves us because we are His children created in His image to give Him glory. The Bible states in II Timothy 1:9, "Who hath saved us, and called us with a holy calling, not according to our works, but according to his own purpose and grace, which was given us in Christ Jesus before the world began." Listen, you can never do anything more or less to have God's love and grace. His love has nothing to do with gender, race, ethnicity, neither based on our human efforts, fragility, weaknesses, or shortcomings.

To me, there is an old hymn "The Love of God" that best describes God's love. It is one of my favorite hymns that ministered to me when I first gave my life to Jesus and it still brings me to tears. It was written by Frederick M. Lehman in 1917. The story behind this song is a very interesting one, so I will share it with you. It has been adapted from Al Smith's *Treasury of Hymn Histories*. [34] Frederick M. Lehman was a California businessman that lost everything in his business. He was forced to spend his working hours doing manual labor by working in a Pasadena packing house, packing oranges and lemons into wooden crates. I am sure this wasn't the place that he would have chosen for himself to be in, but this was the environment the Lord chose to use. Mr. Lehman was a Christian who possessed the joy of the Lord and rejoiced in His salvation. He was so moved by a Sunday evening sermon on the love of God that he could hardly sleep.

The next morning, the thrill of the previous evening had not left him. As he drove to the packing house, the making of a song began to come together in his head, with God's love as the theme. Throughout the day, as he packed oranges and lemons, the words continued to flow. Perhaps he jotted down words on various pieces of broken crates. He could hardly wait to get home and commit these words on paper.

Upon arriving home, he hurried to his old upright piano and began arranging the words and composing a melody to fit them. He soon finished two stanzas and the melody to go with them. But now what was he to do? In those days, a song had to have at least three stanzas to be considered complete. He tried and tried to come up with a third stanza to no avail; the words could not fall into place. He then remembered a poem someone had given him some time before. Hunting around, he found the poem printed on a card, which he had used as a bookmark. As Mr. Lehman read the words, his heart was thrilled by the adequate picture of God's love that they pictured. He then noticed some writing at the bottom of the card.

These words were found written on a cell wall in a prison some two hundred years ago. It is not known why the prisoner was incarcerated; neither is it known if the words were original or if he had heard them somewhere and had decided to put them in a place where he could be reminded of the greatness of God's love. Whatever the circumstances, he wrote them on the wall of his prison cell. In due time, he died and the men who had the job of repainting his cell were impressed by the words. Before their paintbrushes obliterated them, one of the men jotted them down and thus they were preserved.

Lehman went to the piano and began to voice the words with the melody he had just written. They were a perfect fit. It was a miracle! The song was published and remains today with these words as the last stanza. In later years, the origin of these words became known to Alfred B. Smith, which reveals an even greater miracle in the writing of this song. The original third stanza was written in Hebrew around the year 1000 by Meir Ben Isaac Nehoria, a Jewish Rabbi. God, knowing that Lehman was going to write a song, also realized that Lehman would have trouble writing the third stanza and so He chose this rabbi, who although he did not accept Christ as the Messiah, did possess the skills to graphically paint a picture of God's love in words. He would preserve these words and then hundreds of years later, He would have them translated by this prisoner into a language that did not yet exist, namely English. And to think, He did it in the exact meter to fit Lehman's melody! Here are the words to the hymnal below. My prayer is that this song may minister to you as it continues to minister to me.

The Love of God

The love of God is greater far
Than tongue or pen can ever tell;
It goes beyond the highest star,
And reaches to the lowest hell;
The guilty pair, bowed down with care,
God gave His Son to win;
His erring child He reconciled,
And pardoned from his sin.
Refrain:
Oh, love of God, how rich and pure!
How measureless and strong!
It shall forevermore endure—
The saints' and angels' song.
When hoary time shall pass away,
And earthly thrones and kingdoms fall,
When men who here refuse to pray,
On rocks and hills and mountains call,
God's love so sure, shall still endure,
All measureless and strong;
Redeeming grace to Adam's race—
The saints' and angels' song.
Could we with ink the ocean fill,
And were the skies of parchment made,
Were every stalk on earth a quill,

And every man a scribe by trade;
To write the love of God above
Would drain the ocean dry;
Nor could the scroll contain the whole,
Though stretched from sky to sky.

His Love Is Free
I always thought that you have to be good and have to earn love, but this ideology is not true because with God it is free. When I first got saved, I use to say there has to be a catch, there must be some test I have to take, or some blood I have to donate, nothing is for free, that was what I was taught growing up. I was always told that everything cost something, no one just gives you anything in life without expecting something in return. With God I proved that to be a lie, He sent His most precious gift which was His son to die for my sins, and it cost me nothing, but it cost Him everything. The price has already been paid for you at Calvary. There's no list of "If you do this, then I will love you." [35]Charles Spurgeon was a notable preacher from England. He had a powerful calling on his life and said it the best with these two quotes: "This is the glorious, the suitable, the divine way by which love streams from heaven to earth, a spontaneous love flowing forth to those who neither deserved it, purchased it, nor sought after it." He also said, "God's heart, not mine, is the measure of his giving; not my capacity to receive, but his capacity to give." God's love has nothing to do with our mood or our works; it is unconditional and eternal. God doesn't change His mind on you; He knows the mistakes that you were going to make before He sent His son Jesus to die for us, but yet He still sent Him. No matter what you have done, the hurt that you've endured, no matter how many tears you've shed, Jesus is full of grace, mercy, and most of all, compassion. I borrow this quote from [36]Charles Spurgeon:

"Perfect stability belongs alone to God; he alone, of all beings, is without variableness or shadow of a turning. He is immutable; He will not change. He is all-wise; he need not change. He is perfect; he cannot change."

If you ever felt that you were screwed up, you're not the only one—trust me! Growing up, I felt secure knowing that I had a mom and dad. I thought everything was normal—until the enemy invaded my house and I felt like my entire world was shattered. When my father walked out on our family, that decision destroyed my being; I was driven by pain because I didn't know the love of Jesus or what it means to have Him in your life. My father was my world, he was my everything, he was my rock, and was supposed to be in my life forever. I was a daddy's girl. I loved my dad. I adored him and looked forward to seeing him. I was like a little puppy every day waiting at the door and sometimes I was counting the hours for him to come home. However, I didn't know that I had a heavenly Father who would always be true and faithful to me and also to you.

God is so in love with you. You are His first choice. You are not His plan B or C, and to God, you are not an afterthought. The first chapter in the book of Jeremiah expresses that God knew us before we were even in our mother's womb. We are no stranger to God; he knew us long before we have knowledge about ourselves and He has ordained our lives. I had to get the revelation that God loved me with no strings attached and that there was nothing that I can do to get more love or receive less love. He loves us, not for what He can gain from us, for the word of God says that, in Him, all things consist. He loves us for His good pleasure, for what He knows we can become and how he would influence our lives. God also says in Psalm 40:3-4 "And he hath put a new song in my mouth, even praise unto our God: many shall see it, and fear, and shall trust in the Lord. Blessed is that man that maketh the Lord his trust, and respecteth not the proud, nor such as turn aside to lies."

You may be facing a very tough situation, but God will give you a new song. Why don't you take a few minutes and write your new song? Pray and ask God to download words to your new song in your new season.

Take some time and meditate and pray and write your new song below:

Here is my song _____

_____

_____

_____

_____

_____

_____

_____

_____

_____

Chapter 5:
Steps to Your Deliverance

This chapter will cover steps that you must take if you want to be delivered from any demonic forces that are attacking your life. You don't have to continue to be bound by the lies of the enemy. You don't have to stay defeated, but you can overcome through the word of God. I am going to share with you some steps that I had to take to get my deliverance and be free from the spirit of depression, anxiety, low self-esteem, pride, bitterness, molestation, and a few more other demons that God delivered me from.

Accept God into You Heart
The Bible says there is only one way to heaven. Jesus said in the book of John 14:6, "I am the way, the truth, and the life: no man comes unto the Father but by me." The only way is to accept Jesus Christ as your Lord and Savior. The word of God also states in John 3:16–18 (ESV):

> For God so loved the world, that he gave his only Son, that whoever believes in him should not perish but have eternal life. For God did not send his Son into the world to condemn the world, but in order that the world might be saved through him. Whoever believes in him is not

condemned, but whoever does not believe is condemned already, because he has not believed in the name of the only Son of God.

Jesus is our hope and stay. Every plan for our lives can be found in the word of God. Follow God's plans for your life, which have been laid out through the word of God. Jesus is the best thing that ever happened to me. I tried so many things, but all of them brought me pain, regret, sadness, and left me unsatisfied and yearning for more. I had to accept Jesus Christ into my life. I was an atheist, and I didn't even believe that God existed, but I thank God that He saved and set me free. I pray that if you don't know God as your Savior that the power of God does the same for you.

Giving donations to a good cause, baking for your child's bake sale, or attending church once in a blue moon—there are so many things we do as humans to pacify that longing for the presence of God. Good works, alone, cannot save you. True conviction leads to a change of heart and mind. The word of God states, "For by grace, you are saved through faith; and that not of yourselves: it is the gift of God: Not of works, lest any man should boast" (Ephesians 2:8–9).

Faith in Jesus can save you. Wherever you are, all you have to do is accept Jesus into your heart. Sometimes we want to have our own way, but it must be according to the word of God. Please don't wait till you are at the end of life or go around the mountain a few times before you accept Jesus. Through prayer, invite Jesus into your heart to become your personal Lord and Savior. All you have to do is call upon Him. Romans 10:13 states that "For whosoever shall call upon the name of the Lord shall be saved."

Be Willing to Change Your Mind and Repent

I had to be willing to change my mind and turn from my wicked ways and repent from my sins. I hit rock bottom, as people would say. I was an empty shell just going through the motions, I was so unhappy. I had to ask God to forgive me for all that I had done. I wonder if you are at a place where you are tired of relying and depending on your own strength and realize that in knowing Jesus Christ you have everything. That was the supernatural work of the Holy Spirit. The Holy Spirit caused me to no longer have the desire for clubs, alcohol, my promiscuous lifestyle, and the anxiety that was weighing me down. Jesus said, "I tell you, nay: but, except ye repent, ye shall all likewise perish" (Luke 13:5). I didn't want to lose my soul to the devil, it was the Holy Spirit that opened my eyes to see that I was perishing. Most importantly I felt the love of God in my heart, and I pray that God will shine His light upon you. Repentance simply means "to turn," and what brings you true deliverance is when we repent. God knows when we are serious, and we are truly sorry.

Admit that You Need Deliverance, That You Need to Be Free

I learned that God cannot forgive the sin that I wasn't willing to confess. Perhaps, you have some sin in the past that has remained unjudged and unconfessed. You may be committing a sin right now that you do not think is bad. We need to pray as the psalmist prayed, "Search me, O God, and know my heart; try me and know my anxieties; and see if there is any wicked way in me, and lead me in the way everlasting" (Psalm 139:23–24). When we are honest with God in our prayer life, we will have success. The word of God says, "The effective, fervent prayer of a righteous man avails much" (James 5:16).

I had to acknowledge and admit that I was a sinner and that I needed God's help. "Sinner" means that you are not living your life according to the way God intended you to live or according to what the Bible says. I couldn't stop the drinking and smoking habit on my own. I couldn't stop sleeping around and defiling my body; I needed the power of the Holy Ghost to free me from all those demonic spirits. I had to admit my faults—the ones that people saw and the ones that were hidden in my heart. The Bible tells us the following:

> "For all have sinned, and come short of the glory of God;" (Romans 3:23).

> "Wherefore, as by one man sin entered into the world, and death by sin; and so death passed upon all men, for that all have sinned:" (Romans 5:12).

> "If we say that we have not sinned, we make him a liar, and his word is not in us" (1 John 1:10).

> "If I regard iniquity in my heart, the Lord will not hear" (Psalm 66:18).

> "Your iniquities have separated you from your God; and your sins have hidden His face from you" (Isaiah 59:2).

Believe that Jesus Christ died for you, was buried, and rose from the dead.

> "For God so loved the world, that he gave his only begotten Son, that whosoever believes in him should not perish, but have everlasting life" (John 3:16).

"But God commends his love toward us, in that, while we were yet sinners. Christ died for us" (Romans 5:8).

Humble Yourself and Submit unto the Will of God
I had to give up my ways and submit myself under the leadership of Jesus Christ. I had to realize that I was filled with pride; I had to take off the mask. The Webster dictionary states that humility is "freedom from pride or arrogance." We need to get rid of our stubborn and prideful nature.

God is great and His love is infinite. He is the King of Kings, the Lord of Lords. He controls the entire universe and can sustain us. Humanity is frail. We are so limited. Our breath, our heartbeat, our bodies, and everything that we have is because of God. I had to acknowledge that I am not in control; instead, God is. The word of the Lord says, "Humble yourselves before the Lord, and he will exalt you" (James 4:10) and "God resists the proud but gives grace to the humble" (James 4:6).

With everything that has taken place in my life, I've come to realize that we could be here today and gone tomorrow; God is the one that is keeping us alive and He deserves all the glory and praise. I don't know about you, but I don't want God resisting me, and I need all the grace I can get. I also want to receive as much grace as possible. How do I receive grace? It is by humbling myself before the Lord. We can get sick, die, get into a car accident, or even lose our jobs, but God cannot change nor fail. If Jesus was able to be humble, then we can too. This passage of scripture is one of my favorite scriptures (Philippians 2:5–11):

5: Let this mind be in you, which was also in Christ Jesus:
6: Who, being in the form of God, thought it not robbery to be equal with God:

7: But made himself of no reputation, and took upon him the form of a servant, and was made in the likeness of men:
8: And being found in fashion as a man, he humbled himself, and became obedient unto death, even the death of the cross.
9: Wherefore God also hath highly exalted him, and given him a name which is above every name:
10: That at the name of Jesus every knee should bow, of things in heaven, and things in earth, and things under the earth;
11: And that every tongue should confess that Jesus Christ is Lord, to the glory of God the Father.

The good news is that when you humble yourself, God promises that he will exalt you. If you want to receive God's grace uniquely, seek to humble yourself in the sight of God consistently. It is so important to have a good relationship with God so that, through the Holy Spirit and by reading the word of God, He will reveal His mind to us. He is a great God and there is absolutely no one like Him. That is why all glory and adoration belong to God.

Remove the Trash in Our Spirit
So many things come in our way of seeking the face of God. Some are distractions, but some are just trash that needs to be removed from our lives. The Bible speaks about it's not what goes into us that defiles us but what comes out of us. The Bible also talks about the works of the flesh that can hinder us from being in the presence of God. Galatians 5:19-21 "Now the works of the flesh are evident: sexual immorality, impurity, sensuality, idolatry, sorcery, enmity, strife, jealousy, fits of anger, rivalries, dissensions, divisions, envy, drunkenness, orgies, and things like these. I warn you, as I warned you before, that those who do such things will not

inherit the kingdom of God." You see there isn't a good athlete that doesn't look at his opponent or learn about their tactics. So, the Lord has given us His word so that the enemy doesn't trick us with his lies and bamboozle us with his offers. So here are some of the trash that may be dwelling deep in our spirits:

Lack of faith: God can't work with unbelief. We need to believe that what God says in His word is true and that He is faithful to His promises. You must believe in who God is. He can do wonders in our lives if we only believe in Him. Here are some scriptures to use when your faith gets weak or when you feel like giving up:

Hebrews 11:1 Now faith is the substance of things hoped for, the evidence of things not seen.

Hebrews 11:6 But without faith it is impossible to please him: for he that cometh to God must believe that he is, and that he is a rewarder of them that diligently seek him.

James 2:1-26 My brethren, have not the faith of our Lord Jesus Christ, the Lord of glory, with respect of persons.

John 9:35 Jesus heard that they had cast him out; and when he had found him, he said unto him, Dost thou believe on the Son of God?

John 5:24 Verily, verily, I say unto you, He that heareth my word, and believeth on him that sent me, hath everlasting life, and shall not come into condemnation; but is passed from death unto life.

The Spirit of Perfectionism
Some things may not be trash, but they are what is called spiritual clutter, such as the spirit of perfectionism. We need to become so comfortable with who God made us to be, so that we can overcome this spirit. You matter to God, even though the world says that we will never match up with everyone else, and we will never meet the high demands of the world, but what matters is who God called us to be and our purpose in God's kingdom. The bible states in Hebrew 12:1 "Wherefore seeing we also are compassed about with so great a cloud of witnesses, let us lay aside every weight, and the sin which doth so easily beset us, and let us run with patience the race that is set before us," Perfectionism is unattainable. The spirit of perfectionism is a weight. It becomes so heavy sometimes which leads to frustration and is actually an insult to God. We need to understand that it is God's grace that has enabled us to survive through this journey called life. You cannot try to take the place of God in your life, He is our Creator!

If you often stress about trying something new, if you are critical with yourself, if you are always frustrated because you don't feel you got it right, then you need to ask God to deliver you from this spirit. You have to allow God to be the Lord of your life. God has uniquely wired you to be who you are because God knew exactly how He wanted you to be. It's okay to fail, it's okay to try again, and it's okay not to get it right on your first try. Get up and try again. You're not stupid, you're not a failure, you learn and grow and overcome. You are brave and courageous, and failing is also a part of success. Once you let go of your superficial narrative, allow God to tell your story that He has already written and planned for your life, humble yourself and you will find a place of peace. This spirit, which makes you feel that you have to get everything right all the time, is of the enemy, and the root of it is pride. The only one that is perfect is God. You have to denounce this spirit. I had to lay it before God and asked God to remove it from my life. The passage of scripture that helped me overcome this spirit was in Psalms 139, and I hope that this helps you too.

Psalm 139:1-4
1 O lord, thou hast searched me, and known me.
2 Thou knowest my downsitting and mine uprising, thou understandest my thought afar off.
3 Thou compassest my path and my lying down, and art acquainted with all my ways.
4 For there is not a word in my tongue, but, lo, O Lord, thou knowest it altogether.

God knows us all the things that we share and the things that we keep as secrets. God knows exactly who we are, and this has helped me to be honest and true with God. God is all knowing and absolutely nothing could be hidden from Him. I want to be completely dependent on God and not myself. I've learned that as long as I continue to try to be perfect, God will never have room to reveal Himself through me and to me. It's also exhausting trying to be perfect, and you don't have the ability of enjoying the moment, because you are going to second guess yourself and it keeps you self-reliant instead of relying on God. This has caused a lot of people to backslide because they believe the lies of the enemy that things would be better if they were in the driving seat, but that is a lie. God has the best plan for your life. The bible states in Jeremiah 29:11 "For I know the plans I have for you," declares the Lord, "plans to prosper you and not to harm you, plans to give you hope and a future."

Sometimes people are struggling with the spirit of perfectionist because they have an unrealistic picture Of God. That was my issues. Some want to avoid embarrassment because they might have gotten something wrong. They became embarrassed. Now you've made up in your mind that you will never allow anyone to see you making a mistake, but all of that is just one simple word and that is pride. God is not a person who has a big stick and waiting for you to fail to say, "you see I told you that you would fail", no He is our loving Father, He loves us in spite of our failures. This is such a stressful way to live. Every decision doesn't have to be the right decision, some people struggle with what type of cream that they want in their coffee and they are so fearful to make a decision, so they stay stuck. Any decision that we make will give us an opportunity for growth and for struggle. You have to lean into God and trust that the Lord will lead you in life. Take it as an opportunity to learn, to grow and to increase your capacity. Stop getting caught up in being right because life is passing you by.

God used so many imperfect people throughout the Bible for His glory. When I began to learn about King David, and other generals in the Bible and how God still used them and loved them most importantly. Please note that God wants us to be holy, but on the cross, He paid for your past, current and future sins. You are more valuable than your failure. The Apostle Paul said that he asked God three times to take away the thorn in his flesh. He begged Jesus to take it away, but God didn't he gave him Grace instead. He told Paul. II Corinthians 12:9 "And he said unto me, my grace is sufficient for thee: for my strength is made perfect in weakness. Most gladly therefore will I rather glory in my infirmities, that the power of Christ may rest upon me." When Apostle Paul got the revelation that it's that thorn that he is experiencing which is allowing God to manifest His glory through him. Paul's perspective changed and not the situation. Sometimes God doesn't change the situation, but He does change our perspectives. God changed my perspective with this spirit when I was hospitalized right before my graduation. I had so much that I wanted to do before I left on a girl's trip to Dominican Republic. I was set, and was planning for months and when I was admitted for several days I realized that I am not in control of anything because I was hooked up to an IV and had to depend on the nurses and doctors to take care of me, I also realized that life can go on without me.

There are people who get upset because they got an A instead of A+, I wasn't that person. Know that the spirit of perfectionism will cause you to procrastinate and get nothing done because you are waiting for everything to be perfect. Please note that you must learn from your mistakes and failures because people will prefer to stay with "the good you." Otherwise, you will hardly find a crowd that will stay with "the ugly you," full of insecurities and shortcomings. I learned that God loves me regardless of whether I am good, bad, or ugly. He loves me and He loves you too—no matter what!

Be kind to yourself and pay attention to your thought-life. Every day you wake you must remember that you are a winner. Be patient with the process. You didn't just get all these afflictions and negative thoughts overnight, so allow God to process and give you the deliverance that you need. Let your thoughts be pure. The word of God says in Philippians 4:8, "Finally, brethren, whatsoever things are true, whatsoever things are honest, whatsoever things are just, whatsoever things are pure, whatsoever things are lovely, whatsoever things are of good report; if there be any virtue, and if there be any praise, think on these things." Grace is the thing that God has given us to get through those times when we get it wrong.

This spirit is completely different than obtaining and working towards a spirit of excellence. We see in the book of Daniel that he had an excellent spirit. "This this Daniel was preferred above the presidents and princes, because an excellent spirit was in in him; and the king thought to set him over the whole realm."– Daniel 6:3. [37]Jon Courson's commentary mentions, "Darius realized there was an "excellent spirit" within Daniel. What was this excellent spirit? The Holy Spirit. Daniel interpreted dreams. He prayed with effectiveness. He understood visions. He moved in prophecy. He experienced the miraculous. In other words, he was a man who was filled with the Spirit. That's what made him so successful all the days of his life. In 2 Chronicles 16:9, we read that the eyes of the Lord go to and fro throughout the whole earth, looking for a man in whom He might show Himself strong, whose heart is perfect toward Him. Our Father is still looking for men and women in whom He can show Himself strong–as He did with Daniel."

You may ask, "Why is she saying this?" There was a season in my life that I wasn't kind to myself; I would beat up on myself up. A lot of times, I was very hard on myself. I wasn't speaking life over my life and I believed the lies of the enemy for a season. I had to learn how to embrace my failures. Failure doesn't mean your life has ended; it is just an opportunity for growth. I had to learn that I am not my failures, nor do they define me. My failures were just a moment in my life, not a death sentence. I had to ask God to remove that spirit of perfection because only He is perfect, and when I am weak, that is when God is strong! You should desire to have an excellent spirit and get rid of the spirit of perfectionism.

The Spirit of Unforgiveness
You see at some point in each of our lives we will need forgiveness because none of us are perfect. Romans 3:23 "For all have sinned and come short of the glory of God;". We were all sinners at some point, and we needed God's mercy and forgiveness. Now I am not oblivious to the fact that there are some betrayal's, trauma

or violations that we face in the hands of others that can be very difficult to overcome, but just know you can't forgive with your own strength, you will need the grace of God. When our natural mind it's hard to imagine how does a woman forgive a man who's murdered her child, or a husband forgive someone who has hurt his wife, they can't do it without the Holy Spirit? This author by the name of Harold S. Martin wrote, "the greatest forgiveness of all—is an act of God, by which He releases sinners from judgment, and frees us from the divine penalty levied because of our sins. But forgiveness is also a human act toward one's fellow human beings. God's forgiveness, because of the death of Christ in our behalf, is to become an incentive for us to forgive others who offend us."

Peter had a very interesting question to ask Jesus in Matthew 18:31-35 "Then came Peter to him, and said, Lord, how oft shall my brother sin against me, and I forgive him? till seven times? Jesus saith unto him, I say not unto thee, Until seven times: but, Until seventy times seven." The man that hasn't been regenerated may never understand this concept of mercy. The Webster dictionary states that mercy is "compassion or forgiveness shown toward someone whom it is within one's power to punish or harm." Now the Bible dictionary states that mercy is " That benevolence, mildness or tenderness of heart which disposes a person to overlook injuries, or to treat an offender better than he deserves; the disposition that tempers justice and induces an injured person to forgive trespasses and injuries, and to forbear punishment, or inflict less than law or justice will warrant." When we understand that the very foundation of our freedom was based on mercy on mankind. Mercy is what we earned through the death, burial and resurrection that we didn't deserve. And if God can send His only begotten son to die for our sins so that we can be redeemed by the curse of sin, we must find it in our hearts to forgive others.

All throughout scripture we see that Jesus is clearly against the spirit of unforgiveness. It is so important to God that we forgive that he mentions that if we do not forgive our brother, we are not even worthy to pray. Mark 11:25 " And when ye stand praying, forgive, if ye have ought against any: that your Father also which is in heaven may forgive you your trespasses." (KJV). Just take a minute and think about how many times we need God's forgiveness and not matter how bad he situation is, God is able to pardon us. Think about it: Jesus had to forgive us for our many sins, so we need to pardon the people who have hurt us. Ask the Lord to help you because you want to be free from everything that can hinder your relationship with Christ. So, we should always consider ourselves to be conduits of God's grace and mercies toward the people we meet throughout life.

Many times, we try to justify why we are holding on to unforgiveness but it's poison. It's toxic to the heart and to the soul. Unforgiveness causes stress and can lead to physical ailment and illnesses. Sometimes we even hold grudges and keep malice to try to punish the other person or better yet to get them to feel the pain that they caused us, but this only makes us unfruitful in the long run and enables us to be in the fullness of God's glory and presences.

I remember when I just got saved, I struggled with the spirit of unforgiveness, towards my father for leaving us and the people who molested me. The spirit of unforgiveness planted a seed in me when my father left. I thought that he would always be a rock in my life, but this wasn't the case. I struggled with this word: forgiveness. I am not telling you that this spirit was demolished over- night, no it took time, it took countless nights in prayers, I had to rely on God and the Holy Spirit to help me to forgive my dad and the people in my life that I trusted and abused me. I realized that the spirit of unforgiveness was toxic to the soul;

it leaves no room for the Holy Spirit to work. Unforgiveness will keep you stagnant and it will slowly diminish your relationship with God.

I was able to get the revelation from God that this was the weight that was wearing me down emotionally and spiritually. I had to let it go if I wanted to live in God's abundance of joy. I realized that it was preventing me from bearing any fruit in my life. The spirits of unforgiveness and bitterness is of the devil. Bitterness is a deceptive spirit that has the ability to take up a deep root in your soul that will slowly diminish and demolish your destiny. You may say, "You know what? I am done with her" or him, or that job or that relationship, but if you haven't forgiven, it's not truly over. You have to forgive and let it go to be truly free from the spirit of bitterness. You have to forgive so you can be free and move on with your life. Unforgiveness is poison to your soul. It literally kills you inside out. Forgiveness is like taking strong medicine. When you're taking it, it tastes terrible, but once it's taken, you feel so much better than before.

However, you have to forgive yourself first and then forgive all the "others." You see, I had to forgive myself for the many mistakes that I made when I was a sinner. I had to forgive myself for all the things that I did that were shameful and the sexual immorality that I am not proud of. I had to forgive myself for people that I hurt in the past and things that I said that I regret. The "others" are your critics, your haters, abusers, and naysayers. You are not a victim—you are victorious. The Bible says in John 13:34, "A new commandment I give unto you, that ye love one another; as I have loved you, that ye also love one another." In order for you to be able to love, you have to release everything and everyone that is toxic in your life.

You may say to yourself, "Oh, they don't deserve forgiveness. You don't know what that person did to me or what they said about me." All of those thoughts may the facts, but they are not the truth that we are told in the word of God. I know it may be difficult and must have caused you a lot of heartaches but remember that each of us has done something wrong in our lives that needs God's forgiveness. Forgiveness is a God thing and not something that we can achieve on our own. Just remember when you need mercy and forgiveness and ultimately, we want to become a reflection of the word of God through our lives.

Here are some scriptures that through the Holy Spirit will Help you forgive:

Ephesians 4:32–And be ye kind one to another, tenderhearted, forgiving one another, even as God for Christ's sake hath forgiven you.

Matthew 6:15–But if ye forgive not men their trespasses, neither will your Father forgive your trespasses.

1 John 1:9–If we confess our sins, he is faithful and just to forgive us our sins, and to cleanse us from all unrighteousness.

Matthew 18:21-22 Then came Peter to him, and said, Lord, how oft shall my brother sin against me, and I forgive him? till seven times

Matthew 6:14-15 For if ye forgive men their trespasses, your heavenly Father will also forgive you:

James 5:16–Confess your faults one to another, and pray one for another, that ye may be healed. The effectual fervent prayer of a righteous man availeth much.

Luke 6:27–But I say unto you which hear, Love your enemies, do good to them which hate you,

Luke 6:37–Judge not, and ye shall not be judged: condemn not, and ye shall not be condemned: forgive, and ye shall be forgiven:

Colossians 3:13–Forbearing one another, and forgiving one another, if any man have a quarrel against any: even as Christ forgave you, so also do ye.

Proverbs 10:12–Hatred stirreth up strifes: but love covereth all sins.

The Spirit of Selfishness

Me, myself and I, is the way that most people live their lives. God doesn't want us to only consider ourselves, our children, our marriages, and our home. He wants us to care for the poor, the less fortunate. He wants us to have a compassionate heart for everyone, for people that are sick, and to love and cherish our neighbor. Salvation is a selfless act that was done for all of mankind on the cross at Calvary, so Jesus Christ wants to use you as a vessel that he can use to spread his love and kindness towards the world.

Life is hard, so it so easy for us to get consumed in our own lives. It is so much more rewarding to help others. I always enjoyed serving others. I remember when I was attending Catholic school and I believe I was in the second grade and the nuns would give the children breakfast and they said that they were looking for volunteers. As young as I was, I knew that that is what I wanted to do, I wanted to serve. I had a passion for serving. My mom never had to wake me up and I would bug my dad every morning to get me there for 6:30am to prep the breakfast with the nuns for the kids coming in. I was so happy doing it, so serving others I believe is in my DNA. For some people this may not come naturally but you still can ask God to give you the heart of a servant, there is absolutely nothing that God cannot do for you. Jesus, who is God, said that He didn't come to this world to be served but to be a servant to mankind. Be very careful of having an attitude where you need people to constantly serve your and cater to your needs, no we are all placed on this earth by God to serve in which ever capacity that you can. Some people think that it is a less popular thing to be a servant but being a servant is the most rewarding thing that you will ever do in your life. It brings joy and fulfillment to the soul.

Your attitude, intentions, and motives are important to God. He is concerned about the reason that is behind the things that we do and why. Attitude is so important to God. You see in the book of Genesis; we witness the very first sibling rivalry and the first murder between Cain and Abel. The Bible tells us that Abel's offering was accepted while Cain's was rejected. This made Cain angry and upset and his heart started to get corrupt. He became bitter, jealous and allowed himself to be deceived by the enemy in so much so that he killed his own brother. This is why it is so important not to allow these demonic spirits to have any foothold in our lives, they are devilish and destructive. We need to denounce them out of our hearts and minds through the blood of Jesus. Our actions are measured by God because we see in I Samuel 2:3 "Talk no more so exceeding proudly; let not arrogancy come out of your mouth: for the LORD is a God of knowledge, and by him actions are weighed". The part that says, "by Him actions are weighed", means that God examines everything. People have invented these security systems like the one we go through at the airports especially after what took place at 911 in New York City the entire world has increased their traveling security and even though these security measures have been heightened, people still still seem to get through with some unlawful items and that is why they have police officers with watch dogs, well God beats all of that. He can supernaturally scan our hearts and see if we are truly pure in heart. Many actions which are thought to be good in the sight of man, but when God searches man, they are not found perfect before God. Which simply means that somehow, they've allowed negative feelings and thoughts consume their hearts.

The word of God in Luke 6:45 says "A good man out of the good treasure of his heart brings forth good; and an evil man out of the evil treasure of his heart brings forth evil. For out of the abundance of the heart his mouth speaks." (NKJV) From this passage of scripture we see how Jesus is teaching his disciples and followers how to judge a person's character.

Jesus had so many different methods of teaching His disciples. The Gospel is a simple Gospel because He wants everyone to be saved. Jesus often taught by using a parable, that served as metaphors symbolizing life's lessons. In this chapter in Luke, Jesus uses a tree as a metaphor for what really happens in a person's character. Jesus tells us to observe on how we can tell if a tree is good or bad. He said in His word no good tree can bear bad fruit, and a bad tree cannot bear good fruit. If you want to know what kind of tree a person has planted in their heart is very easy just look at the fruits that they bear. Always remember it is what is on the inside of a person will always determine what fruit they produce. God wants us to produce the fruits of the spirit which can be found in the book of Galatians chapter five. When we pray, we have to consider that we are praying with the right heart and the right motive. "When you ask, you do not receive, because you ask with wrong motives, that you may spend what you get on your pleasures" (James 4:3 NIV). One of my favorite passages of scripture is in the book of Proverbs and will give you a better understanding of how important our motives and intents are important to God.

Proverbs 16:1-4
The plans and reflections of the heart belong to man,
But the wise answer of the tongue is from the Lord.
All the ways of a man are clean and innocent in his own eyes and he may see nothing wrong with his actions,
But the Lord weighs and examines the motives and intents of the heart and knows the truth.
Commit your works to the Lord submit and trust them to Him,
And your plans will succeed if you respond to His will and guidance.
The Lord has made everything for its own purpose,
Even the wicked according to their role for the day of evil.

How can we examine our motives, if they are of God or not:
- Ask God to show you if your motives lines up with His word.
- Ask God to show you if your motives are from a pure heart.
- Ask God to show you the real reason why.
- Ask God to show you if your thoughts are from you or from Him.

- Ask God for His wisdom, and instruction on how to deal with the matter.
- Ask God to give you strength to give up your motives, intents, and desires and replace them with His will for your life.
- Ask God to help you to completely surrender and depend on Him because He knows what's best for you and He is intentional!

When we pray for God to use us, is it for His glory or our own? Whenever we pray with a hidden motive, God doesn't get the glory. For example, you can't pray for someone to get saved so you can have someone to marry or pray that your boss loses his/her job. That is why we need to repent; the word says in Acts 3:19, "Repent ye therefore, and be converted, that your sins may be blotted out when the times of refreshing shall come from the presence of the Lord." Our prayers have to be according to the word of God.

Here are some scriptures to help you overcome the Spirit of Selfishness:

Philippians 2:4–Look not every man on his own things, but every man also on the things of others.

2 Timothy 3:2-4–For men shall be lovers of their own selves, covetous, boasters, proud, blasphemers, disobedient to parents, unthankful, unholy,

1 John 3:17–But whoso hath this world's good, and seeth his brother have need, and shutteth up his bowels of compassion from him, how dwelleth the love of God in him?

1 Corinthians 10:24–Let no man seek his own, but every man another's wealth.

Philippians 2:3-4–Let nothing be done through strife or vainglory; but in lowliness of mind let each esteem other better than themselves.

1 Corinthians 13:4-6–Charity suffereth long, and is kind; charity envieth not; charity vaunteth not itself, is not puffed up,

Philippians 2:21–For all seek their own, not the things which are Jesus Christ's.

Galatians 6:2–Bear ye one another's burdens, and so fulfil the law of Christ.

Romans 15:1-3–We then that are strong ought to bear the infirmities of the weak, and not to please ourselves.

Having Idols in Our Lives

I know you might be thinking, "I don't have shrines in my house. What is she talking about?" Idolatry is anything that you put before God. Anything or anyone that is in your life that you treasure and is the first thing or person you think about when you wake up and the last thing or person that is on your mind before you go to bed your idol. Matthew 6:21 says, "For where your treasure is, there will your heart be also." Treasures are considered to be any object, idea, philosophy, habit, occupation, sport, or loyalty that, to any degree, decreases one's trust in God.

My idols used to be my looks, my friends, the clubs, and weed. It could be your car, your job, your children, or yourself. The word of the Lord said in Matthew 6:33, "But seek ye first the kingdom of God, and his righteousness, and all these things shall be added unto you." Try not to let anything come before God in your life.

Denounce the Demonic spirit That Has Been Oppressing You

You have to denounce that spirit. The Merriam-Webster dictionary says that the word "denounce" means to publicly declare something to be wrong or evil. I was carrying so much guilt, and the devil was tormenting me with my past, telling me how dirty, filthy, and guilty I was. I had to confess to my Pastor the things that were troubling me from my past: the guilt and shame that the enemy was using to torment me. I had to tell them to Jesus through prayer, that the real me wasn't loveable. I struggled with this until I started talking about my past with my Pastor and she gave me some scriptures to meditate on, which helped me a lot. I also started to open my mouth in prayer and confess my sins to God; I began to feel better. The Bible says the following:

James 5:16: Confess your faults one to another, and pray one for another, that ye may be healed. The effectual fervent prayer of a righteous man availeth much.

I John 1:9: If we confess our sins, he is faithful and just to forgive us our sins, and to cleanse us from all unrighteousness.

Proverbs 28:13: He that covereth his sins shall not prosper but who so confesseth and forsaketh them shall have mercy.

Read Your Bible Every day to Know Christ Better
Every relationship to get stronger and better requires work. For a relationship to grow stronger there must be communication, commitment and intimacy. The only way we can know who God truly is and that is through His word. The Bible is our guide and tool to use in order for us to stay on the right path to eternal life. God's word is perfect—it cannot change. That is why you have to use it as your number one source of protection and to find your joy.

Reading the word of God helps you to live a Godly life. While I was in Jamaica on a mission's trip during our daily prayer Rev. Dr. Delroy Chambers was leading that day and he made a very profound statement that about the word of God. He said, "No Word, no breakfast, No Word, no lunch, No Word, no dinner!" so what he was saying is that the word of God is more needed then the natural food that we eat for our bodily nourishment. I appreciated this statement so much. The word of God also tells us in Luke 4:4, "And Jesus answered him, saying, it is written, that man shall not live by bread alone, but by every word of God." The devil even attempted to try to tempt Jesus, who is the son of God. If the enemy can try to attack Jesus could you imagine what he will try to do with us.

I find my joy through the word of God. The Bible was the first book that I enjoyed reading, I fell in love with the word of God and it has been keeping me through life. God's word is Eternal.

The word says:

2 Samuel 22:31: As for God, his way is perfect; the word of the Lord is tried: he is a buckler to all them that trust in him.

Psalm 18:30: As for God, his way is perfect: the word of the Lord is tried: he is a buckler to all those that trust in him.

2 Timothy 2:15: Study to shew thyself approved unto God, a workman that needs not to be ashamed, rightly dividing (aligning and applying) the word of truth.

Psalms 119:105: Thy word is a lamp unto my feet, and a light unto my path.

Matthew 24:35 Heaven and earth will pass away, but my words will never pass away.

Psalm 119:89 Your word, LORD, is eternal; it stands firm in the heavens."

It is very important to be in a church where you are being fed with the word of God. I am so grateful to my Pastor and church family. It was the Bible studies and the prayer meetings that helped me come out of my depression. If I didn't have a church family, a community, and the support, I don't know how I could have got through- some of the roughest seasons in my life.

Here are some things, God, that I denounce from my life as of today:

1._____
2._____
3._____
4._____
5._____

Chapter 6:
Scared, But Do It Anyway!

"Fear is a weapon that you have the power to break"
—Dr. Cassandra Altenor

Listen it is a natural thing to experience fear, but when it becomes crippling, that type of fear is unhealthy. Fear and anxiety are spirits that come from the devil. Fear will rob you of the blessing that God has for you. The word of God says in II Timothy 1:7, "For God hath not given us the spirit of fear, but of power, and of love, and of a sound mind."

There are different types of fear—the fear of not being good enough, fear for the future, fear of dying, etc. For example, I always wrestled with the fear of not being good enough. Sometimes our emotions fluctuate like the stock market, but I trust in God's consistency. The spirit of fear and anxiety always comes to torment. We often deal with the spirit of fear by pacifying it with something else, like shopping, gambling, drinking, having illicit affairs, secret addictions, or making up excuses to keep the spirit of fear and anxiety with us.

I believe that fear steals our joy and keeps us away from our destiny. The spirit of fear can leave us crippled, paralyzed, and bound from doing the things that God has put in our hearts or what He destined us to do.

We must live in our present and not in our past because God already has it under control. The word of God states in Philippians 4:6-7, "Be careful for nothing; but in everything by prayer and supplication with thanksgiving let your requests be made known unto God. And the peace of God, which passeth all understanding, shall keep your hearts and minds through Christ Jesus."

We worry so much about our future and often can't let go of our past, but if God can provide for the lilies that don't work, how much more His children, He can take care of us. Half the time, the things that we spend countless nights worrying about don't happen and we just waste time thinking when we should be sleeping. He just wants us to be obedient and faithful servants.

Panic and anxiety are forms of the spirit of fear. According to the Mayo Clinic, [38] "a panic attack is a sudden episode of intense fear that triggers severe physical reactions when there is no real danger or apparent cause. Panic attacks can be very frightening. When panic attacks occur, you might think you're losing control, having a heart attack, or even dying." [39]

Have you ever experienced waves of panic when you think about how your life should be? Common thoughts that could come to mind include "You should be engaged!" "You should be pregnant!" "You should have been further in life by now!" "You should have graduated from college by now!" "You should have been promoted by now!" Social media doesn't help the situation at all.

I suffered for a long time from panic attacks and it got really bad when I was away in college. It was so critical, I stayed in bed because I was scared of not succeeding or doing well in my exams. The fear was crippling. My belief is that we no longer live below our God-given privilege and inheritance, and we will live in the fullness of God's grace and mercy.

However, I've learned that fear limits our ability and vision. It serves as blinders to seeing what a few steps down the road and it may be just delays us from fulfilling our assignment. When the enemy can't get us to fear, he will get us to worry, and when that doesn't work, he will make us doubt what God has told us. He is so crafty. That is why we must learn how to know the voice of God.

The Christian journey is valuable, and believing in our God-given talents, abilities, and self-worth can empower us to walk down a brighter path. Yes, I was scared of going to those volleyball tryouts, and I felt like everything within my body was shaking like a tsunami, but I went anyway. My mind was bombarded with so many negative thoughts, but I pushed and went. Fear can be crippling, but I pushed beyond fear or how I felt. Finally, I summoned courage and went for it. I was scared, but I did it anyway!

The work of the spirit of fear is to magnify the lies of the enemy; it is designed to dilute the truth and fabricate a lie in our mind. The enemy wants to defuse the truth about the word of God. We have to counteract fear with faith and the word of God. The truth and power that lies in the word of God are compared to none.

Another time in my life when I was crippled by the spirit of fear and anxiety was when I was a freshman in high school. It was significant because we just moved to New Jersey, my father had left us, and I had to start public school. I suffered from the spirit of anxiety for a long time. For example, when I was thirteen years old, I had this dream every night where I was standing over a coffin and when I got closer to the coffin, it was my mother. I saw my sisters across the casket, and I was thinking about what I was going to do. I was so scared in the dream, and then I would wake up. Night after night, I would have the same dream. The enemy was trying to plant that seed of fear in my subconscious mind.

It wasn't until I got saved that I realized that the enemy had put a spirit of fear because my father left, and I had developed some serious abandonment issues. The enemy wanted me to believe that I would be left with no one in my life and I would be all alone as an orphan. These were all lies from the enemy. You see that feeling was so overwhelming, I was afraid of speaking in front of others and I was afraid of failing. I was fearful of people's opinions about me. I didn't even know that God had a calling on my life at the time, but I knew I was very fearful and desperately wanted to be free from that spirit.

My church was invited to this Saturday-night revival in Brooklyn. I was seeking God earnestly to get rid of this feeling and didn't know that my deliverance was about to be manifested that night. God supernaturally removed that fear from me, and I've never felt that again. It was gone, deliverance came for me, and I believe that it's going to come for you too. You see sometimes, the enemy will try to tell some of you that you're not saved because you have issues that you are still struggling with, but God is a deliverer. Just keep praying and seeking God. I didn't know, but God knew that He was going to use me, and I needed to be free and not bound. Now I worry less and worship more!

Throw Fear Away

It's time to throw fear away and ask God to set you free and give you peace in your life. How can you beat the fear factor? You can beat fear with the word of God. The word says in I Peter 5:7, "Casting all your care upon him; for the careth for you." Now let's examine other Bible versions on the same verse:

1 Peter 5:7, NIV: "Cast all your anxiety on him because He cares for you."

1 Peter 5:7, ESV: "Casting all your anxieties on him, because He cares for you."

1 Peter 5:7, NASB: "Casting all your anxiety on Him, because He cares for you."

1 Peter 5:7, NLT: "Give all your worries and cares to God, for He cares about you."

1 Peter 5:7, HCSB: "Casting all your care on Him, because He cares about you."

Peter is telling God's children to throw fear away. The word "cast" means to throw it. What we must do with fear and anxiety is to throw it on Jesus. Yes, take your worries, anxieties, and fears to God, who is 100 percent interested in you having joy and peace. We have to trust Him with the good and bad things in our lives. Trust me, He can handle it!

Apostle Peter was giving us a command and not making a suggestion. So, stop holding on to it and cast your cares upon the Lord. I can boldly say that God delivered me from the spirit of fear, and He will for you too. Don't get me wrong. There are still some things that make me feel fearful, but now I pray over those things and no longer suffer from anxiety and panic attacks. I am free! Oh, hallelujah! Praise God, I am free! God can also give you freedom.

The Bible tells us over and over we must not fear. Fear not!

Scriptures to Help You Overcome the Spirit of Fear

Isaiah 41:10: "Fear thou not; for I am with thee: be not dismayed; for I [am] thy God: I will strengthen thee; yea,

I will help thee; yea, I will uphold thee with the right hand of my righteousness."

Isaiah 41:13: "For I the LORD thy God will hold thy right hand, saying unto thee, Fear not; I will help thee."

Deuteronomy 31:8: "He will never leave you nor forsake you. Do not be afraid; do not be discouraged."

Deuteronomy 31:6: Be strong and of good courage, fear not, nor be afraid of them: for the LORD thy God, he it is that doth go with thee; he will not fail thee, nor forsake thee.

2 Timothy 1:7 "For God hath not given us the spirit of fear, but of power, and of love, and of a sound mind."

1 John 4:18: "There is no fear in love; but perfect love casteth out fear: because fear hath torment. "He that feareth is not made perfect in love."

2 Timothy 1:6-7: "Wherefore I put thee in remembrance that thou stir up the gift of God, which is in thee by the putting on of my hands."

Romans 8:15: "For ye have not received the spirit of bondage again to fear; but ye have received the Spirit of adoption, whereby we cry, Abba, Father."

Hebrews 13:6: "So that we may boldly say, The Lord is my helper, and I will not fear what man shall do unto me."

Isaiah 35:4: "Say to them that are of a fearful heart, be strong, fear not: behold, your God will come with vengeance, even God with a recompense; he will come and save you."

John 14:27: "Peace I leave with you, my peace I give unto you: not as the world giveth, give I unto you. Let not your heart be troubled, neither let it be afraid."

Exodus 14:14: "The LORD shall fight for you, and ye shall hold your peace."

Psalms 23:4: "Yea, though I walk through the valley of the shadow of death, I will fear no evil: for thou art with me; thy rod and thy staff they comfort me."

Psalms 27:1: "The LORD is my light and my salvation; whom shall I fear? The LORD is the strength of my life; of whom shall I be afraid?"

Psalms 55:22: "Cast thy burden upon the LORD, and he shall sustain thee: he shall never suffer the righteous to be moved."

Romans 8:28: "And we know that all things work together for good to them that love God, to them who are the called according to his purpose."

Hebrews 4:16: "Let us therefore come boldly unto the throne of grace, that we may obtain mercy, and find grace to help in time of need."

Today, I would like to challenge and ask you these questions: What is that thing that is keeping you from moving forward? What is that thing that is making you feel fearful? It might be the fear of losing your job, a bad doctor's report, fear of death, or fear of losing a loved one. Whatever it may be, God is your strength. You are not facing this fear by yourself—the Holy Spirit is your comforter, and He will give you the courage and grace that you need to face the spirit of fear. Just take a few seconds and fill in below everything that makes you fearful:

These are the things that makes me fearful:

1._____
2._____
3._____
4._____
5._____

Repeat these words: God, I bring these things that make me fearful. I cast them upon you today, God. I need supernatural release and I declare divine deliverance in my life in Jesus's Name!

You see, the only thing that can remove your fear is to have faith. The word of God says, "Faith cometh by hearing and hearing the word of God." When you read the word of God and believe it, your faith will begin to grow. The enemy is intimidated by your future and destiny and this is why he tries to infiltrate your life with the spirit of fear. He is seriously nervous about your position of authority. That is why he wants to blind your mind, your thought life, your mental capacity, and your emotional life. Joy is a heavenly commodity. He endured the cross because He wanted to give you His joy. You are not trying to get victory. Change your perspective. You are in a position of authority through the Holy

Ghost and you already have the victory through the blood of Jesus Christ over two thousand years ago. "For the kingdom of God is not a matter of eating and drinking but of righteousness and peace and joy in the Holy Spirit" (Romans 14:17 ESV).

God is on your side and you have nothing to fear! It doesn't matter who leaves you, who forsakes you, who rejects or disappoints you. God will never leave nor forsake you. Some of the worst times and moments in my life, when I was in my valley and in a dark place emotionally and physically, was the time I felt that the Lord was closest to me. It was in those moments that I give thanks and I'm grateful that I am saved. Isaiah 65:24 says, "And it shall come to pass, that before they call, I will answer; and while they are yet speaking, I will hear." It is also in those moments that God comes running to our rescue.

God's Not Ready for Your Demise
Last year, I went on a mission trip to aid my Pastor with another branch that the Lord led her to establish. During that time, everything was going fine, I was doing everything that I was assigned to do, and it was such a blessing. I always knew that I wanted to do God's work and serve His people. My prayer for many years has been for God to open a door for me to be in full-time ministry, and as I patiently wait, every opportunity that I get to share the gospel with God's people is such a joy.

On New Year's Eve, I went home after service and had some chicken that evening. The next day, I woke up in a cold sweat and experienced one of the worst stomach pains that I've ever felt in my life. I felt like I was literally going to die. I thank God for the angels that He had with me in the house that helped me get up, although even with the help, I kept feeling worse as the hours passed. Every minute felt like an hour and every hour that passed felt like it was an entire day. I didn't know where I was or who was around me. I was weak, I was throwing up, and I felt the spirit of death. Then Overseer Kingsley, his wife, and his sister Opal began to pray for me, and I felt a little better. I thank God for the Welsh Family that was there for me during the mission trip during this entire ordeal. Sis Joan, Overseer Kingsley, and Opal were able to find a doctor that was open on a holiday and rushed me there.

When the doctor saw my dilemma, he rushed me into his office and gave me some medicine. All I did at that time was cry out to God for help. I cried unto God because I knew He had the power to bind the spirit of death. I just declared Psalms 118:17 over my life: "I shall not die, but live, and declare the works of the Lord." I just kept on repeating this verse.

Although the enemy was afflicting my body, I knew that I couldn't die at that moment because God led me to go on this mission trip. I was confident that God would protect me from every harm and danger because of His word. The word of God says in Psalms 34:19, "Many are the afflictions of the righteous: but the Lord delivereth him out of them all." I knew that God would deliver me. I didn't share with my Pastor or family the severity of my illness. I felt only 10 percent better, but a few hours later of receiving treatment, I started having the same symptoms. The next day, I had to go back to the doctor's office because I wasn't feeling better.

The doctor sent me for more tests at a radiology center that was just next door, and while I was there, an elderly woman came out of the office in a wheelchair for a test. She was on her way back to the doctor's office. When I went back to the doctor's office, I saw her family crying and screaming, "She's dead!" The lady had died right there. I felt really bad for their loss because I saw that they were heartbroken they were. The enemy tried to put fear in me by having me in that office to witness the lady's passing, but I said "Devil, not today." I repeated the scripture "I shall not die."

I don't care if you are surrounded by things that are dying. The truth is that if God is not ready for you, the devil cannot kill you.

The Secret Place of God
Every day after that event was a struggle physically and emotionally, but I declared this: "God, I am doing your work and I believe that you are going to keep me alive." When you're feeling fear in a distressful situation or facing emotional challenges, turn to Jesus. No matter what, His promises are sure. He is on your side. Don't listen to the devil's lies; you are not alone because God is with you. God is saying, "You will be okay. I'm all you need and you're never going to be alone because I am with you." I experienced a season of testing and serious warfare, but I am here today because Jesus kept me.

I felt like I was dwelling in the secret place of God. The Bible says in Psalm 91:1, "He who dwells in the secret place of the most High shall abide under the shadow of the Almighty." The very essence of God is His love. This secret place is where we meet with God one-on-one; it is where we should find ourselves. When we abide in God, we find shelter, refuge, and fortress. It is in the secret place that we are most vulnerable with God and it's when we are vulnerable to God that we experience His intimate love.

Here are some things that take place in the secret place:
1. **See Your True Reflection Mirror**: The true you manifest, removing all the walls that you've worked so hard to build up.
2. **Surrender**: You see how little you are and how *big* God is. You realize that there is not much (or practically anything) you can control in life; you come out of the driver's seat. You realize that whatever you've been manipulating or trying to fix on your own is a waste of energy and time, especially when God has the final say in our lives.

3. **Be Real:** You lose the need to appease, pretend, or put up a pretense. You tell Jesus the real you and give your real name.
4. **Hear from God:** You are able to get heavenly frequency and Hear from God directly.
5. **No Fear:** All fear and anxiety are removed and replaced with His sweet presence and peace. You will find incredible strength to overcome some of life's toughest moments in the secret place.

You must understand that God does not test us because He wants us to suffer or prevent us from fulfilling our destiny or obtaining eternal life. He put us through tests so that we can develop a godly character, which is necessary to remain in Him through our good and bad times, through thick and thin. In short, the secret place is not for the lazy or the weak because you have to work to get the results. The secret place is a place reserved for people who love God and obey His word.

Conquering the Spirit of Intimidation with Praise
After you conquer the spirit of fear, you have to tackle and deal with the spirit of intimidation and the voices of the enemy that you hear in your head. Yes, honey, those voices that sometimes magnify themselves when you are on that hospital bed, when you are having conflict at work, and when your marriage seems like it's hanging on a string. Trust God and His process.

This spirit of intimidation is designed by the enemy to stop your progress and sabotage your destiny. The devil is angry when you begin to differentiate his voice from God's voice. The Bible states in John 10:27, "My sheep hear my voice, and I know them, and they follow me:" Don't follow the voice of the enemy, your circumstance, or your environment. Just follow the voice of God. He is the author and the finisher of your faith.

The King James Version of I Peter 5:8 says, "Be sober, be vigilant; because your adversary, the devil, as a roaring lion, walketh about, seeking whom he may devour." But I like the New International Version, which says, "Be alert and of sober mind. Your enemy the devil prowls around like a roaring lion looking for someone to devour." Just know that the enemy doesn't play fair; his assignment and intention is to kill and destroy us. He is a schemer; he creates chaos where there is peace and tries to create hate where God has placed love and joy. That is the secret: you can silence the roar with praise!

Let us get back to my volleyball tryouts. The enemy started speaking lies, telling me that I wasn't as good as the other girls trying out. The enemy was telling me that I had no balance, I was clumsy, and couldn't spike. It went on and on throughout the entire week, but I just pushed my way through.

Yes, he was playing that comparison game with me. How many of us have gone through that comparison game? When you compare yourself to others, it is just like you're telling God that He didn't do a good job on you. You are exactly who God wants you to be. You have the right height, hair color, tone of voice, body type, etc. You are authentic, perfect just the way you are because you were made in God's image to bring Him glory!

The first tryout cut was on Wednesday and then a second one I believe was on Thursday. I continued to perform awfully during the practices. I fumbled and missed the ball several times, but I was hoping that my coach wouldn't notice. Based on the lies that the enemy was telling me, I was convinced that I didn't make it.

So, when I made it, I was shocked and also scared of what was to come. Further on in the book of I Peter 5:9, the Bible states, "Resist him, standing firm in your faith and in the knowledge that your brothers throughout the world are undergoing the same kinds of suffering." You are not the only one going through suffering, struggles, or disappointment. We all have our battles and trials to face, but we have a heavenly Father who is watching over us. You have to take the chance and get the push to try. My prayer is that you will get the nudge and the push of the Holy Ghost to pursue your dreams and passions.

From the time that I was in kindergarten, I was the tallest girl in my class until I got into high school. I was cool with it until I started hearing people call me light post and giraffe. Yeah, I was picked on, but back in the day, all we did was laugh at each other. But beneath the laughter, a seed of doubt and a lack of self-confidence started to develop in me. I started to think that something was wrong with me because I wasn't the same height as all the girls in my class. I began to think that I wasn't good enough, not knowing that God doesn't make anything average.

There is a similar story in the Book of Numbers, Chapter 13 where Moses and the Israelites reached a place called Kadesh Barnea. Moses chose a man from every tribe, including Joshua and Caleb, and asked them to go and spy out the Promised Land. You see, before Moses could conquer the land, he had to decide on his military tactics. He needed accurate information about the land, so he depended on these twelve spies to make serious decisions. The twelve spies reported back that the land was fertile and flowed with milk and honey, but it was well-fortified. But the word of God says that because Caleb had another spirit, he stilled the people. This means that Caleb had an excellent spirit and he believed God's word. Caleb stopped the people from making negative confessions and he refused to continue with the negative words that were being released by the other ten spies. Caleb stopped them from telling bad news to their leader Moses. The people even complained and wanted to choose another leader and return back to Egypt but going back was not an option.

You have to make up in your mind and in your spirit that you are not going back to being depressed, oppressed, and sad. Joshua and Caleb appealed to the Israelites to trust in God's protection. But the people were ready to rebel. Moses explained to them that God was angry with their rebellious ways and that "Not one of them will see the land that He promised to their ancestors except Joshua and Caleb" (Numbers 14:23). All the spies who explored Canaan—except Caleb and Joshua—were struck down by a plague and died. It is important for you to be obedient and get rid of all the negativity in your life.

One day during the volleyball tryouts, the coach made us do only jumps and squats. I was thinking "This doesn't make sense." She made us do so many squats that I didn't feel like getting up in the morning because of the pain in my calves. At the time, I didn't understand that I had to develop that muscle and strengthen my calves because I was going to need them to be able to jump to block the spikes.

Could it be that the pain that you are going through is what God is using to develop the level of spiritual strength that you're going to need for your destiny? The more we rely on our lack or shortcoming, the less our faith grows. You have to trust in Him more than in your friends, job, degree, mate, etc. So, my coach said, "When you see that ball coming, just jump and keep your two hands together and when you see the other team setting someone else for a spike, get yourself in position and get ready to block. Keep your eyes on the ball and follow the ball." I am urging you to believe and follow God!

You see, the thing that I grew up thinking disqualified me—being tall—was the very thing that qualified me to be on the team. God has called you with everything that you need to move into your destiny and calling. The word of God says in Matthew 22:14, "For many are called, but few are chosen." One day, I was watching

Scared, But Do It Anyway!

this YouTube video about a lady who decided at the age of fifty-five to become a bodybuilder. People may have thought that her time had passed and that she is crazy, but you should see her now at seventy-five—she looks like a twenty-five-year-old! With God, all things are possible. Don't let the enemy limit or paralyze you with the spirit of fear and intimidation because you can do all things in Jesus's Name.

Here are some of the things that makes me fearful:

1._____
2._____
3._____
4._____
5._____

Chapter 7:
Don't Get Bitter—Get Better

Some of you have experienced some bitter waters, when you get bitter waters, want to throw them away. Do not throw a drop of it away, for that is the water you have yet to drink. Accept your afflictions. They are a part of your education.
—Charles Spurgeon.

I know that when you read this next statement I am about to share; you're probably going to say this lady is crazy! I am about to say something so crazy right now and I just want you to let it simmer.

Having pain is a good thing!

Yes, I said it is a good experience. Pain is an indicator that you're alive. Now, I know you're probably saying other things can make you know you're alive. But pain is an indicator that there is something you need to deal with, something that you have to deeply look into and figure out what's wrong. When God saved me, He allowed all the pains that I had left deeply rooted and folded neatly in the deepest compartment of my soul to come out; all of it was brought to the surface. Yes, that is what the Holy Spirit does. God deals with our internal pains, conditions, and afflictions.

I recently spoke to a nurse and she indicated that nowadays, people get addicted to medications, but it does not fix their problem; it is just a temporary solution. This is what sin was doing to my life: the drinking, clubbing, fornicating, and smoking were just temporary fixes, not permanent solutions. But the moment I said yes to God, things began to surface, and God began to heal me.

Throughout life, we have many challenges that involve countless disappointments, betrayals, and rejections, to name a few. Betrayal by someone that you love and thought had the same sentiments about you can be so devastating. It is a type of pain that only God can eliminate from your heart. It is one of the hardest hurts to get over. It is probably the worst feeling in the world. The reason why I can say this is because I have been through this same path in my life. Indeed, this is something that I struggled with and honestly, it was betrayal. I had to constantly ask God for me to forgive people who betrayed my trust. I am glad that Jesus delivered me and took that pain away from me.

I remember when I was in college, I met a young lady and we got really close. She made me laugh and I thought that we were cool. I was dating this guy, but there was just something about him that I didn't trust, and I kept on mentioning it to her. She would tell me to stay with him. "He is a nice guy, give him a chance. I know he really likes you." She was my friend at the time, so of course, I trusted her. I was living off-campus at the time and I decided I would stop by his apartment. When I got to his first-floor apartment, I noticed he had his window open. While the breeze was blowing, I was able to see my so-called friend kissing the guy that I was dating.

Of course, I was in sin: the situation made me fume and I said some not so very nice and unsanctified words to both of them. Some of you have been in marriages where you made vows and promised in the presence of God and thought that you would be together forever and then the same person filed for divorce or you lost them to addictions. All of these things I believe are seeds of the enemy planted in our hearts and souls hoping that it corrupts us and causes us to become callous.

You see, betrayal stirs up all the thoughts and feelings that are not pleasing to God and they just begin to fester. You don't want that. You want to live a free and victorious life in Christ that is free from hatred, anger, rejection, fear, etc. The worst thing to do is to break someone's trust. When I was young in Christ, I trusted everyone because I assumed that if they were Christians and had godly principles, they would always behave in a way that is pleasing to God. But I quickly learned that this wasn't the case. Human beings come stamped, "subject to failure" when they enter this world. God tells us plainly in His word that we cannot put our trust in man. These readings from the Bible are great examples of how to trust God.

> **Micah 7:5:** Trust ye not in a friend, put ye not confidence in a guide: keep the doors of thy mouth from her that lieth in thy bosom.

> **Isaiah 2:22:** Cease ye from man, whose breath is in his nostrils: for wherein is he to be accounted of?

> **Psalm 118:8:** It is better to trust in the Lord than to put confidence in man.

> **Jeremiah 17:5–8-:** Thus saith the Lord; Cursed be the man that trusteth in man, and maketh flesh his arm, and whose heart departeth from the Lord. For he shall be like the heath in the desert, and shall not see when

good cometh; but shall inhabit the parched places in the wilderness, in a salt land and not inhabited. Blessed is the man that trusteth in the Lord, and whose hope the Lord is. For he shall be as a tree planted by the waters, and that spreadeth out her roots by the river, and shall not see when heat cometh, but her leaf shall be green; and shall not be careful in the year of drought, neither shall cease from yielding fruit.

Psalm 62:8: Trust in him at all times, O people; pour out your heart before him; God is a refuge for us.

Overcoming the Spirits of Shame and Condemnation

Some of the things that the enemy uses to keep you bitter are shame and regret. Shame is the feeling that something is wrong with you. It makes you feel like you want to go into hiding. It is said that "The feeling of guilt is about doing something wrong, whereas shame is about being wrong at the core." The feeling of shame comes from the belief that says, "I am basically flawed, inadequate, wrong, bad, unimportant, undeserving or not good enough."

When you have an unresolved feeling of shame, it can open doors to fear, depression, anxiety, and low self-esteem. When a person suffers from shame and regret, it brings condemnation. For example, I carried the load of shame and condemnation for a very long time because as a child I was molested by a family member; I always felt inadequate. Although I didn't completely understand what was going on, I knew that it didn't feel right. As I grew older, the devil planted the seed of shame. So, from an early age, I've been ashamed of myself. When I looked back, I discovered that my behavior was always defensive because I was afraid that people would find out my secret and I was embarrassed. It is not God's desire for us to go through life carrying such a heavy load. We can use the word of God to fight back when the enemy wants to overwhelm us with condemnation. Here are some scriptures that deal with the spirit of condemnation:

Romans 8:1: There is therefore now no condemnation to them which are in Christ Jesus, who walk not after the flesh, but after the Spirit.

John 3:17: For God sent not his Son into the world to condemn the world; but that the world through him might be saved.

1 John 3:20: For if our heart condemns us, God is greater than our heart, and knoweth all things.

Romans 8:34: Who is he that condemneth? It is Christ that died, yea rather, that is risen again, who is even at the right hand of God, who also maketh intercession for us.

John 8:11: She said, No man, Lord. And Jesus said unto her, neither do I condemn thee: go, and sin no more.

Isaiah 35:3-6: Strengthen ye the weak hands, and confirm the feeble knees.

Psalms 40:11-12: Withhold not thou thy tender mercies from me, O LORD: let thy lovingkindness and thy truth continually preserve me.

Romans 8:1-39: There is therefore now no condemnation to them which are in Christ Jesus, who walk not after the flesh, but after the Spirit.

Psalms 34:21: Evil shall slay the wicked: and they that hate the righteous shall be desolate.

Psalms 34:22: The LORD redeemeth the soul of his servants: and none of them that trust in him shall be desolate.

1 John 1:9: If we confess our sins, he is faithful and just to forgive us [our] sins, and to cleanse us from all unrighteousness.

Romans 5:1-21: Therefore being justified by faith, we have peace with God through our Lord Jesus Christ:

Psalms 103:10: He hath not dealt with us after our sins; nor rewarded us according to our iniquities.

Isaiah 43:25: I, even I am he that blotteth out thy transgressions for mine own sake, and will not remember thy sins.

Shame can cause isolation and separation, a situation where you don't want to be around people because of how you are feeling about yourself. You may be suffering from the spirit of shame because you might have gotten a divorce, filed for bankruptcy, committed infidelity, have an addiction, secret lust, and temptations. Others have experienced severe trauma and heartache. Some of you have been carrying this guilt of shame for a very long time and I am telling you that you can be free from that bondage. Shame also causes loneliness. The shame I felt was so crippling and it brought so much fear and torment, but I thank God for the blood of Jesus that was applied to my heart. Jesus made a difference in my life. It was not until I accepted Jesus that the Holy Spirit worked in my spirit, mind, and soul. You can bring all your troubles to the Lord.

My life was transformed, and my soul healed. I had to confess the shame issue to God and I also discussed it with my Pastor because I wanted to be free. You have to be desperate for your freedom; you have to want it bad enough to expose those dark issues in your soul. Through prayer and confession and staying in God's presence, I can boldly say that I am delivered. I no longer carry the shame of my past because I had to learn how to see myself just the way God sees me. The Bible says that I am fearfully and wonderfully made. I believed the word of God by faith that my past will no longer keep me captive. I had to believe the word that says that I am forgiven, and my sins are washed away.

Here are some things that shame will make us subconsciously believe about ourselves:

- I'm a failure.
- I'm not important.
- I'm unlovable.
- I don't deserve to be happy.
- I'm a bad person.
- I'm a phony.
- I'm defective.

These are all lies from the enemy. God knew you before you met your parents, He knows everything that you would go through, and He still chose to send His only son, Jesus Christ, to die for you on the cross. Jeremiah 1:4–5 says, "Then the word of the LORD came unto me, saying, before I formed thee in the belly I knew thee; and before thou camest forth out of the womb I sanctified thee, and I ordained thee a prophet unto the nations."

Don't get Bitter, but get Better!
This has been my motto. Honey, choose your battles! Don't feel as if you've been assigned to fight every fight; you will wear yourself out. When you are complete in God, you will worry less about how others feel about you. When you know who you are in Christ, you will no longer have the desire to prove yourself to others. The enemy will use people to discourage and put false lies in you. The enemy will try to stop and delay you. The enemy will use voices, whether they be internal or external, to make you get bitter. You must guard your heart.

Although I was saved, I was still hearing negative things that people spoke into my life. The word of God says in Luke 22:31, "And the Lord said, Simon, Simon, behold, Satan hath desired to have you, that he may sift you as wheat." I struggled because, as a kid, I often heard about the things that I wasn't good at. For example, I struggled a lot with math, and I could never understand it. But I didn't know that I shouldn't dwell on the negative things that I was told by my parents. I know now that they didn't know the impact that it had on me. I know that they wanted me to do well, but the comments didn't make me feel good about myself.

The enemy will also try to use the strategy of playing comparison games. Another spirit that God had to break off of me which was the spirit of comparison. "Why can't you be as smart as this and that person?" "Why can't you behave like this and that person's daughter?" I truly don't believe it was said with evil intentions, but the impact of the negative words continued to fester into my early adulthood. The spirit of comparison spirit makes you feel that you are not good enough just the way you are. The enemy will have you going around like a hamster on a wheel when you start to compare yourself.

God made you unique. You see, I wasn't taught that growing up. It was my pastor that taught me through the word of God that I am special in God's eyes and He made no mistake creating me. There will always be the temptation to entertain negative thoughts. Isaiah 26:3 states, "Thou wilt keep him in perfect peace, whose mind is stayed on thee: because he trusteth in thee." You have to read and study the word of God so you could know who you are in Christ." It is important to know the word of God so you can counteract these negative thoughts with the word of God. Philippians 4:8-9: "Finally, brethren, whatsoever things are true, whatsoever things are honest, whatsoever things are just, whatsoever things are pure, whatsoever things are lovely, whatsoever things are of good report; if there be any virtue, and if there be any praise, think on these things."

People will put limitations on you, but God says what is impossible with man is possible with Christ. Heaven has already declared it; you just have to speak it. Shut the noise out and put the false voices on mute through His Holy Spirit and stay focused. Speak positive things into your atmosphere. Watch out for those destiny killers that want to take you off course of your destiny through their words of fear and doubt.

Sometimes there will be no one to encourage you, so you have to encourage yourself in the Lord. You have to speak to yourself. For example, David had gone to battle, and when he returned from the war, he found that all his family members were kidnapped. And the men that fought with him? Their families were gone, the town was burned down, and everyone was upset. Everyone wanted to stone David. But David had to speak and also encourage himself. The word said in I Samuel 30:6: "And David was greatly distressed; for the people spake of stoning him, because the soul of all the people was grieved, every man for his sons and for his daughters: but David encouraged himself in the Lord his God." A very tough but necessary lesson to learn is that sometimes, the people that you think will be there to encourage you will not be there when you need them the most. You know why? Because human beings as a whole are subject to failure. We just don't have that capacity to always be faithful only God does. But I know a man named Jesus that the Bible says will never leave nor forsake you. You are God's number one priority. The Bible says in Proverbs 18: 21, "Death and life are in the power of the tongue: and they that love it shall eat the fruit thereof." Stop confessing failure and defeat but confess victory and strength.

"My Lord gives me unlimited credit at the Bank of Faith," said Charles Spurgeon.[40] In God we have unlimited resources of love, health, wealth, strength and whatever you may need in God. I love this quote by Sam Storms: "Joy is not necessarily the absence of suffering; it is the presence of God."[41] Have you ever been driving or walking, and the rain started to drizzle? The initial start is just raindrops, which are no big deal because you can hardly feel them. Then all of a sudden, what seems to be just a small thing becomes severe, as if heaven opened up and there was no water left in it. It's as if God just started to say, "Let's get rid of this water up here!" It just starts gushing. Lightning starts to flash, and darkness bestows the earth. This is what happens sometimes in our lives. The storms seem to come out of nowhere. But God has a plan for every storm. Storms are forms of opposition and opposition creates opportunities for God to develop us.

A few years ago, I was going through some serious warfare, and when it couldn't get any worse on the job, I experienced the loss of a younger sister. Prior to that, I often attended funerals but never understood the gravity of pain the person experienced; I really couldn't relate. Until August 2011. I remember this like it was yesterday.

It was a Sunday afternoon after I had left service when my middle sister called me and said that Jessica was in the hospital and wasn't feeling too good. I figured, "Oh, it's probably minor. She probably is so exhausted from all that studying for her bar exam." I had just attended Jessica's law school graduation a few months prior and I knew that she was studying extra hard. Ever since my sister was six years old, she wanted to be a lawyer. That was her dream. I remember one occasion, when she was about four years old and my parents were having an argument, she took her little hands and covered up my dad's mouth and pointed her index finger for him to shush. My dad moved my mom to the other side of the room and said "Bad! Bad!" They didn't have any choice but to start laughing hysterically. From that day, we knew that she would be different.

Jessica went from being monitored, to an induced coma, and then to cardiac arrest within five days. I prayed and I had people praying. I declared the word of God over her by her bedside. I believed that she was going to make it so much. So, I said that Thursday, "Well, I've been in the hospital all week with Jessie. Let me just go visit a young man named Bro Kyle from my church who was having heart surgery at another hospital across town because I wanted to see how he was doing, it was suppose to be just a quick visit and then I would head back to the hospital and see my sister Jessica. God is so gracious, God kept this young man through that heart surgery and now he is anointed and preaching the Gospel of Jesus Christ. I am grateful that God's purposed prevailed in this young man' life."

As I was getting ready to leave after seeing the young man, my sister Stephanie called and said, "Jessie is in a code red.

Please hurry and come." Jessica passed that day. Paul writes to the church at Thessalonica that "For you received the word in much affliction, with the joy of the Holy Spirit" (1 Thess 1:6) indicating that joy is associated with God the Holy Spirit and that the "righteousness and peace and joy is in the Holy Spirit" (Rom 14:17) and finds it source in God as even "the disciples were filled with joy and with the Holy Spirit" (Acts 13:52). If it wasn't for the Holy Spirit I couldn't get through the loss of my sister.

The Impact of Toxic People
Being around negative people can get you bitter. My Pastor always says, "People are like elevators; they could either take you up or down in life." I love my Pastor; she is filled with so much wisdom. It is very important who you surround yourself with. The people that you allow in your circle can positively or negatively affect you, which can affect your destiny.

The definition of toxic means "involving something poisonous, deadly, lethal, contaminated, venomous, and harmful." These kinds of people know how to turn your sunshine into rain. Constantly being around that negativity can eventually ruin your self-esteem. There are some people that I am convinced are anointed by the enemy to discourage you. Negative people can be very poisonous in your life if you allow them to be. They will make you be insecure and make you doubt yourself. Today take back that power that you gave them over your life. God will send people in your life that will support and encourage you. Have you ever been feeling really good about the day, or got some good news about your life, and one conversation with someone has you feeling low, unworthy, doubtful, hopeless, and out of your element? That is what happens when you have toxic people in your life. There should be a big sign that comes with toxic people that says "Beware" and "Danger." They just know how to shift your mood and change the atmosphere. They drain you and often come with words filled with doubt and fear. Toxic people know how to turn your sunshine into a tsunami, not even a slightly cloudy day. When they come, they come with the thunder and lightning, poles are being dragged down, streets are losing lights, roads are being blocked, the news reporters are calling for evacuation, and I am not joking. I am serious; they are just that negative; they only see the bad ending to the story; they never see the light nor bring hope or encouragement. Slowly but surely, these types of people will steal your joy. They don't rejoice with you, they don't wish you well, they don't support your God given calling or gift. Ask God to help you get rid of these negative people out of your life.

Well, I don't believe that this is the will of God for your life. God will put people in your life that will see God in you and love you for who He has made you to be. It's easy to find support in good times, but I believe that God will have some people in your life that will love you through the good, the bad, and the ugly times of your life. God will also divinely send people in your life that will enhance your walk in Christ. People that will encourage your spirit to hold unto the promises of God. People that will pray for you and intercede on your behalf. God will put the right people at the right time in your life for His glory. Find people that will encourage and support you. A true friend is not constantly taking and not giving. I am not talking about material stuff, but most of the time, I find that the emotional and spiritual support is worth far more than the financial aid. You're not supposed to keep a record, which means if you do this for me, then I do something in return. That is not how God desires for us to be. Friendship should be mutual—both parties should feel supported, honored, and respected. The Bible speaks about friendship in the following chapters below:

Proverbs 18:24: A man that hath friends must shew himself friendly: and there is a friend that sticketh closer than a brother.

Proverbs 27:17: Iron sharpeneth iron; so a man sharpeneth the countenance of his friend.

Proverbs 17:17: A friend loveth at all times, and a brother is born for adversity.

Proverbs 27:9: Ointment and perfume rejoice the heart: so doth the sweetness of a man's friend by hearty counsel.

Proverbs 27:6: Faithful are the wounds of a friend; but the kisses of an enemy are deceitful.

Proverbs 22:24-27: Make no friendship with an angry man; and with a furious man thou shalt not go:

Ecclesiastes 4:9-12: Two are better than one; because they have a good reward for their labour.

John 15:13: Greater love hath no man than this, that a man lay down his life for his friends.

1 Thessalonians 5:11: Wherefore comfort yourselves together, and edify one another, even as also ye do.

1 Corinthians 15:33: Be not deceived: evil communications corrupt good manners.

Hebrews 10:24-25: And let us consider one another to provoke unto love and to good works:

Job 6:14: To him that is afflicted pity should be shewed from his friend; but he forsaketh the fear of the Almighty.

1 Peter 4:8-10: And above all things have fervent charity among yourselves: for charity shall cover the multitude of sins.

John 15:12-14: This is my commandment, that ye love one another, as I have loved you.

Romans 1:12: That is, that I may be comforted together with you by the mutual faith both of you and me.

1 Corinthians 13:1-13: Though I speak with the tongues of men and of angels, and have not charity, I am become as sounding brass, or a tinkling cymbal.

Sometimes, the enemy will use your family or closest friend to bring contention. The enemy knows that it will have the worst impact and that it will be challenging. But still, don't allow the enemy to rob you of your joy. Determine that you won't allow their words to define or shift your atmosphere nor frame of mind. It's the decision you have to make that you will not allow their words to penetrate. I've heard misery loves company and I have proven this saying to be true. Do not give anyone the power to determine when you are happy or sad.

God always loves His people, but His people do not always know it. Because of their sins, they do not always enjoy it. Charles Spurgeon said, "God is up to something even when you can't see it. It will not always be a dark season, but your spring shall spring forth. There is a treasure in you that you need to allow to manifest by believing and trusting God's will for your life." [42]

Stop Caring About What Others Think of You.
God doesn't want you to waste another minute or hour fretting on how you are perceived or what people think of you. God would rather you go through His written word and know He has called you to be. It is just a way that the enemy tries to distract us from seeking the things of God that will enable us to be empowered to do His will and mandate.

Please note that I believe that God will place people in your life that will help assist in propelling you to His divine destiny for your life. And God will place spiritual mothers and fathers in your life to guide and be your covering. People who can discern and are in tune with the Holy Spirit. I am so grateful for my Pastor, who many times rescued me from some of the pits that the enemy had planned for me. The many times that Pastor rebuked me kept me steady through my journey with Christ. She has been a strong tower in my life. I am so blessed and favored to have the opportunity to glean her wisdom and learn so much from her about the anointing—the call, sacrifice, and discipline—that one must endure being used by God.

The rest of the people are just like bees. You see, if you have a few bees buzzing around you, that doesn't really affect you. You can just blow them away. But, once you have several around you, this could be dangerous. Remember how we talked about toxic people in our lives? Use the same application for them.

Surround yourself with strong, spiritual, sound, and wise men and women of God who see the calling on your life. They'll spiritually impart gifts in your life. Men and women of God that will correct you and crush those things that aren't producing good fruits in your life. You can't waste time being everything to everyone!

There are so many God-opportunities that you will forfeit if you are busy worrying worrying about what people think of you. As I mentioned before a few great men and women that were able to do great things, and I am sure that they could not have accomplished them listening to what people had to say about them. I have never heard of people doing great things for God while worrying about what others thought of them. In my own experience, very early in my Christian journey, God removed people that would have distracted me and kept me from His will for my life. He surrounded me with spiritual generals in His kingdom that I was able to learn from, my beloved Pastor and other leaders in my church have shown me the path to God, and I am so grateful for them.

I heard that this man of God once said, "What people think or say about you will not take you to your destiny." Don't miss God because of people's opinions. We stay in unfruitful and perturbing relationships much longer than we should because we are worried about what people will say. We buy things that we cannot afford and live-in houses that we cannot maintain just because of people. It is better to put all that energy into finding out the promises of God in His word and His purpose for your life. The word of God says in 1 Timothy 6:6-7 "But godliness with contentment is great gain. For we brought nothing into this world, and it is certain we can carry nothing out."

Self-Sabotage: You Are Your Worst Enemy
I was doing a study on this behavior 'self-sabotage' and I discovered so many meaningful and important nuggets. I learned that self-sabotage is when you undermine your own goals and values. Most importantly I learned from Nick Wignal [43]that self-sabotaging behaviors can be both conscious and unconscious depending on how self-aware you are of them:

- [44] **"Conscious self-sabotage is when you are aware of the fact that what you're doing is undermining one of your goals or values. E.g.: Remembering that you need to pick weeds in the backyard but deciding to play video games instead."**
- **"Unconscious self-sabotage is when you do something that undermines a goal or value but you don't realize it until after the fact. E.g.: People with a strong fear of failure in their jobs often develop the unconscious habit of showing up late or doing sloppy work as a way to avoid promotions or increased responsibility which would lead to higher expectations and therefore a higher chance of failure."**

The enemy will create endless ways for us to fall into self-sabotage. This is why we have to confess the word and seek God's presence for direction for our lives. The word of God says [45]James 2:20 "But do you want to know, O foolish man, that faith without works is dead?" (NKJV) This just means that you can't have faith alone. I've heard preachers say, "Yea, a man may say, thou hast faith, and I have works shew me thy faith without thy works, and I will shew thee my faith by my works."

It's amazing how it is so easy for us to believe in God's abilities for someone else, but when it comes to us, it is so hard for us to believe. You see, I know for me I can believe and lie before God for someone and intercede for them, but when it comes to me and my personal issues, sometimes doubt and fear come upon me. Lately I've become intentional on what thoughts I allow myself to meditate upon. I have chosen to be much kinder to myself. That's weird right. Sometimes I feel that we beat up on ourselves because we are comparing ourselves to everything but who God says that we are. God created us for His glory and His praise. Jesus throughout scripture always asked the person before they received their healing, "Will thou be made whole?" Which basically means do you want this, you have to want to be at a better place spiritually, and emotionally. It is our belief and our faith in God that will sustain us through life. We must have faith in God and remember that He is our keeper. The word of God says in Hebrew 11:1, "Now faith is the substance of things hoped for, the evidence of things not seen."

We tend to make these defeated and negative confessions and declarations over our lives. "I will never make it." "I am not going to make it." "I am going to fail." It's amazing how we are able to convince ourselves and talk ourselves out of our blessings. The Bible talks about the power that we have in our tongue:

Proverbs 18:21: Death and life are in the power of the tongue: and they that love it shall eat the fruit thereof.

Proverbs 12:18: There is that speaketh like the piercings of a sword: but the tongue of the wise is health.

Proverbs 16:24: Pleasant words are as a honeycomb, sweet to the soul, and health to the bones.

Proverbs 15:1: A soft answer turneth away wrath: but grievous words stir up anger.

Proverbs 13:3: He that keepeth his mouth keepeth his life: [but] he that openeth wide his lips shall have destruction.

Proverbs 21:23: Whoso keepeth his mouth and his tongue keepeth his soul from troubles.

Ephesians 4:29: Let no corrupt communication proceed out of your mouth, but that which is good to the use of edifying, that it may minister grace unto the hearers.

Matthew 15:18: But those things which proceed out of the mouth come forth from the heart; and they defile the man.

Matthew 12:36: But I say unto you, that every idle word that men shall speak, they shall give account thereof in the Day of Judgment

Matthew 12:37: For by thy words thou shalt be justified, and by thy words thou shalt be condemned.

Colossians 3:8: But now ye also put off all these; anger, wrath, malice, blasphemy, filthy communication out of your mouth.

Psalms 19:14: Let the words of my mouth, and the meditation of my heart, be acceptable in thy sight, O LORD, my strength, and my redeemer

Spend Your Time Wisely

Don't waste time focusing on people and things that don't matter. God loves you so much that He choose you to be alive this day and whatever the devil is trying to do in your life, God is bigger than anything that you may be facing or dealing with. You need to consume your energy and time on the things that God would have you to do while you are on earth. Most of the time we rely on things around us to define us, people around us to validate us, but people will fail and will change, circumstances will change, but God will never change. Honor God by honoring yourself and knowing your worth. Don't allow anyone or anything to define you but God.

Sometimes when people lose their jobs, or get a divorce or lose a loved one, the event is painful, but I believe that most of the pain is the psychological lost. It's that feeling as if you've lost your own self or your own identity because it was wrapped up in that person, or in that particular company, in that title. But you need to read the word of God to know your true identity. You're not defined by nothing or no one but God. Don't worry when you hit rock bottom, just look up to God because He can pick you up again. Always remember that if you start on relying someone else to give you joy, you will soon become attached and will begin to rely on that person for your joy instead of God who is your true source of joy. The only one that you truly need, the only one who knows the real YOU! No one that God puts in your life was created to complete you but to compliment His purpose in your life. Here are some scriptures to strengthen your trust in the Lord:

> Trust in the LORD with all thine heart; and lean not unto thine own understanding.
> **Proverbs 3:5**

In all thy ways acknowledge him, and he shall direct thy paths.
Proverbs 3:6

And they that know thy name will put their trust in thee: for thou, LORD, hast not forsaken them that seek thee.
Psalms 9:10

For I know the thoughts that I think toward you, saith the LORD, thoughts of peace, and not of evil, to give you an expected end.
Jeremiah 29:11

The LORD is my strength and my shield; my heart trusted in him, and I am helped: therefore my heart greatly rejoiceth; and with my song will I praise him.
Psalms 28:7

Jesus Christ the same yesterday, and to day, and for ever.
Hebrews 13:8

Though he slay me, yet will I trust in him: but I will maintain mine own ways before him.
Job 13:15

Commit thy way unto the LORD; trust also in him; and he shall bring it to pass.
Psalm 37:5

Thou wilt keep him in perfect peace, whose mind is stayed on thee: because he trusteth in thee.
Isaiah 26:3

> It is better to trust in the LORD than to put confidence in man.
> **Psalm 118:8**

O LORD my God, in thee do I put my trust: save me from all them that persecute me, and deliver me:
Psalm 7:1

We procrastinate and make excuses that disqualify us from God's blessings. There is so much power in our thoughts and words. You can start speaking to yourself and stop agreeing with the lies that the enemies have put in your head. This breath that you have been given by God is precious and should be cherished and not wasted to speak lies. Use your breath to prophesize greatness upon your life and your future. Love the life that God has given you, call old friends, do things that you enjoy, and laugh a lot. God will bring the right people into your life.

Most of the time, the enemy is not your boss, your wife, your kids, or neighbors. Sometimes, the enemy is us! We are critical of ourselves and often believe the lies of the enemy. Some of you have received prophecies and conformations from God, but because you've convinced yourself that the lies of the enemy are true, you haven't stepped out on faith. What people say to you is not as important as what you say to yourself. We can kill our destiny by the words we declare and release in the atmosphere. Spend time with people who respect and appreciate your presence, you weren't an afterthought to God, you should never settle to be an after-thought to anyone.

The enemy lies—and his lies can only be muted by the word of the living God. You want to win the battle? Stay in the word of God. Hide in the word, and you will find peace and refuge. Sometimes, His voice will get so loud, you can't even recognize the voice of God, but the Bible says in John 10:4-5, "And when he putteth forth his own sheep, he goeth before them, and the sheep follow him: for they know his voice. And a stranger will they not follow but will flee from him: for they know not the voice of strangers." Stop giving self-inflicting wounds in your mind, thoughts, life, and speech. Remember that God made you in His image to bring glory to His Holy name.

Forgive Yourself
I have made some bad decisions; I've assumed things about people that weren't true. I've judged wrongfully, I've said things that was hurtful to people that I truly love, I've said things that I regret. I want to be transparent so you can know that you are not the only one who has done something wrong, but God saved me and forgave me for my sins. One of the best things that God did for me was to deliver me from the opinion of others. I struggled a lot with that, but God set me free, and it took away a heavy load off of me when He did that. If the enemy has caused you to fail, or faulter, there is hope in King Jesus. The Holy Spirit has helped me to forgive myself and helped me to realize that this is exactly why we all have to run to the feet of Jesus. I am flawed, and He is flawless. I am imperfect but Jesus is perfect in all His ways. Yes, my God could handle your mess. Only Christ is perfect.

I love the story about King David in the Bible because he had such a penitent heart. David was called by God and loved God, but he had issues. He was real with God and received the mercy and favor of God.

Constantly our prayer should be similar to David's in **Psalms 51:10-19**

> 10 Create in me a clean heart, O God; and renew a right spirit within me.

11 Cast me not away from thy presence; and take not thy holy spirit from me.
12 Restore unto me the joy of thy salvation; and uphold me with thy free spirit.
13 Then will I teach transgressors thy ways; and sinners shall be converted unto thee.
14 Deliver me from blood guiltiness, O God, thou God of my salvation: and my tongue shall sing aloud of thy righteousness.
15 O Lord, open thou my lips; and my mouth shall shew forth thy praise.
16 For thou desirest not sacrifice; else would I give it: thou delightest not in burnt offering.
17 The sacrifices of God are a broken spirit: a broken and a contrite heart, O God, thou wilt not despise.

Here are some scriptures that helped in the season's where I have felt as if God could never use me again. These scriptures helped me overcome the spirit of condemnation:

Romans 8:1 There is therefore now no condemnation to them which are in Christ Jesus, who walk not after the flesh, but after the Spirit.

James 5:16: Confess your faults one to another, and pray one for another, that ye may be healed. The effectual fervent prayer of a righteous man availeth much.

Luke 6:27-28: But I say unto you which hear, love your enemies, do good to them which hate you, Bless them that curse you, and pray for them which despitefully use you.

I believe that the thing the enemy loves is to use the spirit of condemnation. The first thing that you have to do is to forgive yourself. This was a struggle for me during my early years of salvation. The enemy used my past against me and told me lies like:

1. I am not worthy of God's forgiveness.
2. God is going to punish me for what I did.
3. God will always hold it against me.
4. You have every right to be upset with that person.
5. You are a victim and will always be a victim.
6. No one will love you if they find out about your past.
7. What you did was so shameful, God won't forgive you.
8. Hold on to that offense or the events in your past.
9. You don't deserve happiness.
10. You will never get over your past.

Have you ever experienced the feelings of guilt, shame, regret, fear, and unworthiness? These feelings will sometimes lead us to also struggle with the spirit of condemnation most of the time. The lies are from deep wounds in our hearts. Most of the time, these lies are from deep wounds in our hearts. But don't believe these lies from the enemy. People might have attempted to harm you, but the Lord protected and shielded you from your enemies. And when you forgive them, that doesn't mean that they weren't guilty; it just means that you want to be free to allow to move on with your life in God's peace.

Here are some more scriptures on how to deal with the spirit of condemnation. For example, the Bible clearly tells us in Romans 8:1, "There is therefore now no condemnation to them which are in Christ Jesus, who walk not after the flesh, but after the Spirit." When the devil tries to bombard your mind with the sins and mistakes of your past, just remember these few scriptures:

Psalms 34:22: "The Lord redeemeth the soul of his servants: and none of them that trust in him shall be desolate."

I John 1:9, "If we confess our sins, he is faithful and just to forgive us our sins, and to cleanse us from all unrighteousness."

Isaiah 43:25: "I, even I, am he that blotteth out thy transgressions for mine own sake, and will not remember thy sins."

Psalm 103:10: "He hath not dealt with us after our sins; nor rewarded us according to our iniquities."

Ask God to bring restoration to your soul. The Bible says in Psalms 51:2, "Restore unto me the joy of thy salvation; and uphold me with thy free spirit." You need to allow yourself to be transparent in the presence of God. Joy is the expression of God's loving-kindness. Happiness never lasts, but the Bible says in Nehemiah 8:10, "Then he said unto them, 'Go your way, eat the fat, and drink the sweet, and send portions unto them for whom nothing is prepared: for this day is holy unto our Lord: neither be ye sorry; for the joy of the Lord is your strength. That the joy of the Lord is your strength.'"

It is when you pray for the people that have fought against you and pray for your enemies. Don't fall trapped in the snare of the enemy. Failure and the spirit of fear is a trap. Joy is the expression of God's loving-kindness. In the book of Nehemiah chapter 8:10 says toward the end of the scripture, "for the joy of the LORD is your strength." Life is good when you trust in God's word. Jesus died that you might have life more abundantly.

Walking around feeling defeated and beating up on yourself is not living more abundantly. That is to say, don't expect people to bring you joy. Don't give them that power; the joy of the Lord comes from God. God alone gives us joy, not people or material things. Ephesians 2:8 says, "For it is by grace you have been saved, through faith and this is not from yourselves, it is the gift of God." Do you feel like all hope is lost? Christ came to give us everlasting hope and joy in Him, not in man or in our jobs. Life will give you some sour lemons, but through God, we can turn those lemons into sweet lemonade.

As of today, God help me to forgive these things:

1._____
2._____
3._____
4._____
5._____

Chapter 8:
You Have Nothing to Lose

As of today, remove these words "lose and loser"
out of your life because in God, we always win!
—Dr. Cassandra Altenor

There is a story in the Bible that I love. This story took place in II Kings 7:3–20. There were four men who were stricken with leprosy and were left to die. No one care about them or dared to be around them. They were rejects and outcasts. The sickness caused them to be isolated. 2 Kings 7:3 says, "And there were four leprous men at the entering of the gate: and they said to one another, 'Why sit here until we die?'" The gate was a place where a lot of people congregated, so they were snared, and people were laughing at them, mocking them, but in the end, God gave them victory! The place where they were was significant and symbolic of transition. In the olden days, gates symbolized safety and security from the enemy, it was also a place where people were able to come into a town and leave the town.

They were sick, dying, and were considered to be outsiders, but they had nothing to lose. You are still alive, and you are still here to fight another day, so don't give up. I believe these men had to think about it over and over again. They had to look at all sides

You Have Nothing To Lose

of the question until they were convinced that they had to make a move. That's exactly what these four lepers did? They turned the question around in their minds into a statement. "If we go into the city, we will die. If we stay here, we will die." Sometimes, we are afraid to pursue the dream that God gave us because of fear. But you have nothing to lose—God needs you in His kingdom.

You will experience a time, or a season that you will feel like quitting or giving up, but quitting is not an option. I know that you just feel as if you can't make it, and you've been rejected, and you want to quit. The enemy is hoping that you quit, but he is a liar and a defeated foe. With your hope and joy in Jesus Christ you cannot lose.

I watched this beautiful story about a young lady who was a professional runner named Gabe Grunwald. Her story is about perseverance and the power of hope. You see she was diagnosed with a rare form of cancer in her twenties. She met her future husband who was studying to be a doctor. She was in love with her husband and running and to get news like that was devastating, but she decided to live her best life. The documentary stated, [46]"The day after her first diagnosis, she ran her then-fastest time in her best event, the 1500 meters. In 2010, she came in second in the NCAAs, the same year she was given her second cancer diagnosis, this time in her thyroid. The next year, she came in third in the country in the indoor championships. And then in 2012, she missed qualifying for the Olympics by just one spot." Who does that but a person with a made-up mind not to quit? She started a foundation called Brave Like Gabe Foundation which raises money for research and to help cancer survivors live active lives. I remember being at a low place in my life where I felt like giving up, and God led me to watch this documentary. This young lady could have just stayed in bed, but she fought back and gave cancer a good fight. Most people will get a diagnosis perhaps once or twice, but she was diagnosed four times with different forms of cancer. Four times, but she never gave up. She pushed passed the negative thoughts and her fear and decided to liver her BEST life! She pushed passed the negative thoughts and her fear and made a decision to live her best life. One of her quotes that I love to read is "It's okay to struggle, but it's not okay to give up on yourself or your dreams." So, you don't give up on that dream no matter how long it takes to manifest. You may be facing a devasting diagnosis, and incurable diseases. If you are facing some difficult challenges, and have experienced loss just know that Jesus is your comforter, and He is your healer. This is why it is so important to know the Lord as your shepherd, because through the Holy Spirit He is able to guide us and keep us in our valleys. The valley is the place where you have your dark and sad moments.

Some Scripture to Use When You Feel Like Quitting

Psalms 23:1-6:
1 The Lord is my shepherd; I shall not want.
2 He maketh me to lie down in green pastures: he leadeth me beside the still waters.
3 He restoreth my soul: he leadeth me in the paths of righteousness for his name's sake.
4 Yea, though I walk through the valley of the shadow of death, I will fear no evil: for thou art with me; thy rod and thy staff they comfort me.
5 Thou preparest a table before me in the presence of mine enemies: thou anointest my head with oil; my cup runneth over.
6 Surely goodness and mercy shall follow me all the days of my life: and I will dwell in the house of the Lord forever.

Philippians 4:13: I can do all things through Christ which strengthened me.

Acts 20:24: But none of these things move me, neither count I my life dear unto myself, so that I might finish my course with joy, and the ministry, which I have received of the Lord Jesus, to testify the gospel of the grace of God.

John 14:16: And I will pray the Father, and he shall give you another Comforter, that he may abide with you forever;

2 Peter 3:9: The Lord is not slack concerning his promise, as some men count slackness; but is longsuffering to us-ward, not willing that any should perish, but that all should come to repentance.

Psalms 119:105: Thy word is a lamp unto my feet, and a light unto my path.

Galatians 6:9: And let us not be weary in well-doing: for in due season we shall reap, if we faint not.

1 Peter 2:24 Who his own self-bare our sins in his own body on the tree, that we, being dead to sins, should live unto righteousness: by whose stripes ye were healed.

Galatians 6:1-18: Brethren, if a man be overtaken in a fault, ye which are spiritual, restore such an one in the spirit of meekness; considering thyself, lest thou also be tempted.

Hebrews 12:1 Wherefore seeing we also are compassed about with so great a cloud of witnesses, let us lay aside every weight, and the sin which doth so easily beset us, and let us run with patience the race that is set before us,

In 2019 I was sick in the hospital, battling food poisoning. I had just gotten back from a mission's trip, and I just didn't feel myself but, I was determined to complete my assignment. When I got home, I immediately rushed to the hospital and they ran a few tests and sent me home, but a few weeks passed, and I was still getting worst and worst. I decided to go back to the hospital. I was discharged and was home, and then three days later, I had to go right back with pneumonia. I needed God to help me through His Holy Spirit. The battle was more psychological than physical. I was engaging in a serious psychological spiritual warfare. You see, after I got home after recovering from pneumonia, the first night that I reached home around two o'clock in the morning, the enemy just told me, "Do not go to sleep because you won't wake up, and you won't get up." It was a frightening feeling. A crippling feeling of fear came over me. I really felt the spirit of death in my room. I immediately woke up and said, "Devil, in the name of Jesus, come out of my room right now. You have no authority or no jurisdiction, and you are a defeated foe. God is my keeper, and I will be alive in the morning."

You can't be weak in the walk of faith and you have to speak with authority because you can never do it in your own strength, but the Lord which strengthens you. The power of the Holy Spirit and the anointing of God removes all fears of the enemy, and you can command boldly the enemy to flee from your atmosphere, your mind, and your life. Yes, you've got that power and authority through the shedding of the blood of Jesus Christ. The devil has whispered negative words in our ears and planted seeds in our minds. We have to rebuke the voices of the enemy. The only thing that we can use to counteract these lies is the word of God. I thank God for saving me from no longer needing to run after these things that are empty in providing joy and happiness.

These lepers were considered to be at the bottom of life and society. They had lost it all. They had lost their wealth, integrity, and dignity. These four men made a decision: they decided that they were not going to stay with those thoughts until they died. You don't have to have any fear and or doubt once you are in Christ Jesus. You see, the four lepers got to the enemies' territory and realized that they had evacuated the scene. You see, God is so amazing that He caused the enemy to think that there was a mighty army after them and they all ran away, leaving the four lepers to take everything. including riches and jewelry.

Faith is an action word. Having faith requires movement; there is no room to be stagnant in God's kingdom. You see if the lepers just remained there feeling sorry for themselves and having a pity party, they wouldn't be able to play an active role in their deliverance. Jesus wants us to be willing and obedient to His will and His word, and after obedience, we must take action. The lepers made a move, and there was no stopping them. The book of James 2:17 says, "Even so faith, if it hath not works, is dead, being alone." Having faith will make you look silly to men, but as long as you know that the Lord has given you a word, you just need to believe that He will sustain us through the moments that the enemy wants to put fear and doubt. God has given us this example for us to know that we can't allow our limitations, or perhaps our shortcomings or lack of resources, or support prevent us from taking a leap of faith. You can no longer stay on the shallow end of life. You need to take a deep dive into God's presence, and once you enter, just stand firm on the promises of God.

The longer that you remain parked in what I call "The Comfort Zone," the further your destiny is from your reach. You have to fight even when you don't feel like fighting. You have to seek even when you don't see things happening with your eyes. God is working behind the scenes. If you want to walk in destiny, then you need to get uncomfortable. You have to step out on *faith*! The Bible states in Hebrews 11:1, "Now faith is the substance of things hoped for, the evidence of things not seen." You can't stay stagnant; it's time to make a move! It's time for you to step out on faith and say goodbye to fear.

I remember when I came out of the hospital last year after spending nearly a month in there due to food poisoning and pneumonia. I was in between jobs and I wanted to find something that I could do while finishing my degree. At this time, I had my MBA and my doctoral degree, but because I was so weak from being admitted to the hospital for a month, I wanted to gradually go back to work. So, I applied for a babysitting job, being that I was so weak and was only able to work a few hours a week. I went to the interview with the children's grandmother and I thought everything went well. I was waiting for the good news, but she never called me back.

So, with all those student loans and diplomas, I thought to myself, "Cassandra, what was the point? I couldn't even get a babysitting job." I felt like I had hit rock bottom. The enemy plagued my mind for a few days about this and then I decided, "You know what? It's their loss. I am a who God says that I am. I am a child of God and He has the perfect job for me and I am a winner in Jesus's name." I rejected the things that were happening in my life, in my atmosphere, because I stood on the word of God that says in these scriptures:

Matthew 7:7 Ask, and it will be given to you; seek and you will find; knock and the door will be opened to you.

Jeremiah 29:13 You will seek me and find me when you seek me with all your heart.

Isaiah 55:6 Seek the Lord while he may be found; call on him while he is near.

Psalm 105:4 Look to the Lord and his strength; seek his face always.

Deuteronomy 31:8–And the LORD, he it is that doth go before thee; he will be with thee, he will not fail thee, neither forsake thee: fear not, neither be dismayed.

Psalm 34:4 I sought the Lord, and he answered me; he delivered me from all my fears.

Deuteronomy 31:6–Be strong and of a good courage, fear not, nor be afraid of them: for the LORD thy God, he it is that doth go with thee; he will not fail thee, nor forsake thee.

A few weeks afterward, I got a job paying me double what I was making previously before I got sick. The Lord will grant you favor in every area if you sincerely seek His face and meditate on His word. It is critical to maintain your faith in life's darkest hours because Jesus will always show up on your behalf, as long as you are His child.

You Are an Overcomer!

You have power in you! You may feel mentally, physically, or emotionally weak, but God has designed you to be an overcomer. You weren't designed by God to lose, no matter who tells you otherwise. You were designed to win and to conquer. Your goal must be to develop a healthy body, soul, and spirit. God's desire is for you to be whole, which means complete in the fullness of His glory and power. His desire is for you to be consumed and filled with the presence of God and that what is going on around you will never dictate what you are carrying within. No, we can't stop life from happening.

You may not be comfortable with your situation. You may feel that you are all alone. But God is right there with you and He is going to deliver you. Remember the word of God says in John 16:33, "These things I have spoken unto you, that in me ye might have peace. In the world ye shall have tribulation: but be of good cheer, I have overcome the world." You see, Jesus came down to humanity and overcame the world, so He is able to help us get through every trial and test that the enemy may send our way. Colossians 1:26-27 says, "Even the mystery which hath been hidden from ages and from generations, but now is made manifest to his saints. To whom God would make known what the riches of the glory of this mystery is among the Gentiles, which is Christ in you, the hope of glory:" I pray that you will seek God and His presence.

God Will Show Up on Your Behalf

We saw a few years ago when the stock markets crashed that several stockbrokers and financial advisors—men and women who were considered experts in the financial sector— couldn't prevent the crash; no matter their level of educational qualification or degrees, they couldn't stop it. This caused many to fall into a state of depression and some eventually committed suicide due to the pressure of loss during the economic crisis. Sometimes you may feel that everything around you is failing and the burdens that you are carrying are weighing you down. These are the moments when you feel as if you're not celebrated or have many friends.

However, this moment is the perfect opportunity for God to show up in your situation. Jesus had to walk on this earth, and He had to go through the challenges that He knew we would have to face. The word of the Lord said in the book of Matthew 4:1-3, "Then was Jesus led up of the Spirit into the wilderness to be tempted of the devil. And when he had fasted forty days and forty nights, he was afterwards a hungered. And when the tempter came to him, he said, 'If thou be the Son of God, command that these stones be made bread.'" Jesus was fasting for forty days and nights and as soon as Jesus was done, the enemy came immediately to tempt Him, but Jesus overcame the enemy and so can you too. Do not allow the enemy to intimidate you with fear. Know that God has your back. Know that not only does God have your back, know that God knows how to show up on your behalf.

I wonder what things the enemy has told you that has kept you in hiding or depressed. When you are depressed, you stop spending time on yourself, and you just become helpless with simple little things. And you lose your desire to do things for yourself and for your loved ones. But your Father will show up to rescue you. In I Kings chapter 19, it shows us the things that God did for Elijah, things that he should have been able to do for himself, but the Lord knew that Elijah was weak and needed His help. God made him sleep and then God gave him food to eat. God gave Elijah two long periods of good sleep, which gave him rest. God will give us things that will allow us to continue on this journey called life.

How Looking Back Can Destroy Your Future
As Christians, it is important for us to live a thankful life in the consciousness of life's brevity. Looking back in life may be cool, but it can destroy where God is trying to take you. Tucking the special moments in your mind is cool; in the future, you will recall all the humorous adventures, special occasions, tender exchanges, and it will all feel great. I love taking pictures even though my friends will say that I always take these pictures that they never see, but I absolutely love it because it captures a moment that we will never have again, and I like to keep that with me.

On the other hand, remember the story of Lot's wife: Lot and his wife were instructed not to look back when they were leaving Sodom. But she looked back and immediately became a pillar of salt and lost her future completely because of her disobedience. Today, I want to let you understand that you are not exempt; you too can quickly lose your future by looking back at experiences that have caused you sleepless nights, pain, or discomfort. Yes, your past is a big part of you and your experiences help develop character, but these experiences can never be compared to the power that illuminates and truly reveals God's purpose for our lives and also gives us true direction. Only God can guide your future. God gives us a new nature and a new mind, and a new walk. We could only get this guidance through reading God's word and listening to the Holy Spirit. This is also why it is so important to have a prayer life and to have a relationship with God so you could seek him for direction and instruction. If you keep dwelling on from where God already delivered you from, you will lose your future even without even knowing it.

You may have lost direction because of disobedience, but because God is a merciful God, He knows how to put you back on a forward-moving track, the ultimate way to the eternal home. Therefore, you should not dwell in the past. God was there in the past with you and He has elevated you from that level. Through His power, we are able to keep moving forward. The book of Habakkuk speaks about writing the vision and it is important to write the things that God puts in our spirit. Habakkuk 2:2–3 says, "And the Lord answered me, and said, Write the vision, and make it plain upon tables, that he may run that readeth it. For the vision is yet for an appointed time, but at the end, it shall speak, and not lie: though it tarry, wait for it; because it will surely come, it will not tarry." Which simply means what God said that He would do will come to pass.

Don't Look Back
Many people look back in most cases due to material things, fear, or doubt; however, God already has a plan for your life even though it may seem as if He has abandoned you or you can't hear His voice. Remember Jeremiah 1:5: He Knew you before you were formed in your mother's womb. Lot's wife looked back to the material things they left instead of looking into God's plan for her life.

Like Lot's wife, you may view the future as a scary place; you're scared because you lack faith in God's plan and you may even have lost a sense of direction once you think about it, but please remember God's word in Jeremiah 29:11. It says, "For I know the plans I have for you,' declares the LORD, 'plans to prosper you and not to harm you, plans to give you hope and a future"(NKJV).

Your faith in God may be weak, but God will help and intervene. When God told Lot and his family not to look back, He was telling them that everything they needed was ahead. Looking back means you still think about the past. In 2 Corinthians 5:7, it says that for we walk by faith, not by sight. God requires us to always trust in Him, no matter what is ahead of us or the challenges that we are facing. Lot's wife did not believe it. God was also telling her that He had already forgiven her and the entire family. It was over, and God was giving them a new life. It is also the same situation today: God has changed your life by moving you from one point to another—do not ever think of looking back. Everything you need, He already has it prepared for you in the future. You only need to trust and believe Him.

God is telling you the same thing: don't look back. Now is the best time for you to get over the past. There is so much in you that God hasn't revealed yet in you. God has a great plan for your life, and in order for you to possess it and grab what God has for you, you have to let go of your past. God is still the great I Am— not the great I Was—He remains so for eternity. Everything about Him is yes and amen, forever and ever. He provides you with a bright future and a plan. He does not want you to keep looking back; God wants us to live hopeful for the future. He wants us to walk by faith, depending entirely on His provision. Therefore, you should live in the moment and completely encounter the present-day blessings from God. No matter what we tend to face, be it financial difficulties, bills, health problems, or marriage crises, we need to trust and put all our hope on God Almighty. The Bible says in Psalm 55:22, "Cast your burden on the Lord, and He will sustain you; He will never allow the righteous to be moved." God loves you, and He will never forsake you. Trust in Him and He will make you whole in riches and wealth.

No More Excuses: Start and Make a Move!
In the book of John chapter five, we see the occasion: it is a festive season in Jerusalem near the sheep gate at the pool of Bethesda, which was a place where everyone who was sick and wanted healing came because, once a year, the Bible says that the angel would trouble the waters and they would be healed. This was a place where the lame and disabled came hoping to get their

miracle. Although there were so many people who needed Jesus' attention, He was just focused on this one man who had been sick for thirty-eight years. This story encourages me to keep on believing in God. Even though you may have been sick for a very long time, God can still deliver you. I choose to believe that God is greater than any sickness that you are facing. God is greater, He is bigger, and He is stronger than what you are facing today.

That day was that man's day of deliverance. A whole crowd of people came for the same purpose, but Jesus healed that man. He couldn't make any more excuses. He could no longer make excuses; he had to take action. As I said previously, faith is an action word! God will remove all the factors that are making you feel comfortable for you to completely rely on God so that you can follow your dreams. Sometimes He removes relationships, jobs— anything that we use as crutches that prevent us from moving forward in God.

Let me get back to my volleyball story. So, in the tryout, the coach shouted out one word at the top of her voice. You see, she was short in stature but full of power. I had walked out into my high school gym room with my gym clothes and I was just standing there watching all the girls playing. She shouted, "Move! What are you going to do? Just stand there?"

It is said that what we experience in the natural realm can be translated to things that are occurring in the supernatural realm of God. God has given you the gift, the prophecy, and the people that will help give birth to your destiny. Yet, you stay on the sidelines, believing the lies of the enemy.

But I am telling you what to do with what God has given you for His kingdom. Are you just going to stand there? Your dream and destiny won't manifest if you don't put in some sweat, and tears in the game, and it is more than just showing up; the word of God must be activated in your life. Stop and decide today that you will no longer be on the sidelines, watching the life that God intended you to have to pass you by. Most of the time, we get frustrated not because of the devil but because of our disobedience. Frustration comes because we know that we are called for more, but we just sit at the sidelines because of fear. The problem is never with God. We know what we should be doing, but we just get stuck. The Holy Ghost can get you unstuck. There will be so many voices that will speak negativity into your life; you have to make a move! So, it wasn't enough that I got dressed and showed up to the tryouts. I had to make a move.

I was so frightened that I just ran over to her. Those forty-five minutes of tryouts for the volleyball team for the next two weeks felt like the longest time of my life, an eternity. I was slow, I was tired, I was in pain, but I finished. After getting through the pain, I said to myself, "It wasn't that bad after all." As I said earlier, sometimes the most important thing to do is just to start. Start believing in God's word so that your faith can overcome your fears!

Cultivate a Life of Thankfulness
I decide to spend the rest of my days giving God thanks for being alive. I think so many times we forget about God's mercy, forget that He is faithful, and it's easy to find things to complain about, but it is so much more rewarding and impactful on our lives if we maintain a life of praise and thanksgiving. It makes a difference to know that you matter to God and that He loves you. So, just have an attitude of gratitude. Here are some scriptures that have ministered to me throughout my journey with the Lord:

> **Psalms 118:1 KJV** "O give thanks unto the LORD; for he is good: because his mercy endureth **forever.**"
>
> **Ephesians 5:20 KJV** : Giving thanks always for all things unto God and the Father in the name of our Lord Jesus Christ
>
> **Colossians 1:3, 12, KJV:** We give thanks to God and the Father of our Lord Jesus Christ, praying always for you... Giving thanks unto the Father, which hath made us meet to be partakers of the inheritance of the saints in light:
>
> **Colossians 3:17, KJV:** And whatsoever ye do in word or deed, do all in the name of the Lord Jesus, giving thanks to God and the Father by him.
>
> **1 Thessalonians 1:2, KJV:** We give thanks to God always for you all, making mention of you in our prayers.
>
> **1 Thessalonians 5:18, KJV:** In everything give thanks: for this is the will of God in Christ Jesus concerning you.

2 Thessalonians 2:13, KJV: But we are bound to give thanks always to God for you, brethren beloved of the Lord, because God hath from the beginning chosen you to salvation through sanctification of the Spirit and belief of the truth.

Hebrews 13:15, KJV: By him therefore let us offer the sacrifice of praise to God continually, that is, the fruit of our lips giving thanks to his name.

So, choose to worship him and choose to give Him thanks. Let your life reflect the blessings that He has given to you. Speak life, speak success, and speak victory. When you are feeling low in the spirit, just begin to give God thanks for His goodness. Start to just count the many blessings and meditate on these scriptures:

Psalm 24:7 "Lift up your heads, O ye gates; and be lifted up, ye everlasting doors; and the King of glory shall come in."

Psalm 30:5 "For his anger endureth but a moment; in his favour is life; weeping may endure for a night, but joy cometh in the morning."

Romans 5:8 "But God commendeth his love toward us, in that, while we were yet sinners, Christ died for us."

Psalms 28:7 "The Lord is my strength and my shield; my heart trusted in him, and I am helped: therefore my heart greatly rejoiceth; and with my song will I praise him."

Psalms 28:8 "The Lord is their strength, and he is the saving strength of his anointed."

Psalm 25:20 "O keep my soul, and deliver me: let me not be ashamed; for I put my trust in thee."

You have to cultivate a life of thankfulness, which means to acknowledge the many gifts that God has given you. It is important for us to be grateful for the small and big things He does for us. When I had pneumonia and it was so hard for me to breathe, something that I never had to think about before getting sick. Now, I give God thanks for being able to breathe on my own. I thank God for being able to walk, talk, look at the skies, and so much more. I am so grateful for life and knowing that as long as I am alive, I have hope in God.

There is nothing like having the peace of God. What is peace? Well, the Merriam-Webster dictionary says it is "freedom from disturbance, tranquility, the absence of conflict or war." But in Hebrew, it means so much more. The Hebrew word *shalom* or "peace" is taken from the root word *shalam*, which means "to be safe in mind, body, or state." It speaks of completeness, fullness, prosperity, harmony, or a type of wholeness that encourages you to give back. It can be used idiomatically to mean both hello and goodbye. Only God can give us peace. You are comforted when you know that you are walking in God's precepts and you also know your purpose in God and His kingdom.

After you have obtained God's favor by accepting Him into your heart, you must then ask God this question: "What is Your purpose and Your will for my life?" In order for you to know God's purpose for your life the first thing that you must do is pray. Ask God to reveal Himself and His will for your life. Ask God to give you wisdom and direction. James 1:5 states, "If any of you lacks wisdom, let him ask God, who gives generously to all without reproach, and it will be given to him." You see, God speaks to a young prophet named Jeremiah and he tells him in Jeremiah 1:5, "Before I formed thee in the belly I knew thee; and before thou camest forth out of the womb I sanctified thee, and I ordained thee a prophet unto the nations." God knew this young man and he knows every one of us and He has an amazing plan for our lives.

God's purpose and vision for our lives can be revealed in many ways. A lot of times, you will feel it in your heart, or God will reveal it to your leader or a prophet, and He will use His word to reveal it to you. It is very important that as you are trying to seek God for His purpose for your life that you be very cautious who speaks in your life, and who counsels you. I am so grateful for my Pastor, who saw that God had a calling on my life and was able to teach me in the ways of the Lord.

The word of the Lord speaks of godly counseling. This is so important for you to have godly counseling. One of the things that I am grateful for is that God gave me a powerful leader who hears from God, and it has been a blessing. You have to remember God has a plan as is said in Jeremiah 29:11, "For I know the thoughts that I think toward you, says the Lord, thoughts of peace and not of evil, to give you a future and a hope." We must also remember that the devil has a plan for our lives also because the Bible says in the beginning of John 10:10, "The thief does not come except to steal, and to kill, and to destroy..." But the latter part of this same scripture is about the victory that we have through knowing Jesus Christ. It says, "I have come so that they may have life, and that they may have it more abundantly. Jesus has no limit in the richness of His grace and mercy and He desires for His children to be blessed and live an abundant life."

Ultimately, in order for us to find what is our purpose in God, we have to literally submit our will and our own agenda and become obedient to the Holy Spirit. When we make Jesus the center of our lives, we find peace, joy, and contentment. You know that you are in the purpose and will of God when you are doing something that comes very natural for you and it doesn't feel like you're working hard to achieve it. Things that come naturally to you as far as your talents and gifts. Don't take your skills and talents for granted: God has given his children gifts and talents for His glory and for His kingdom. Sometimes, God has already given us a vision, but we blow it off or make excuses on why we can't possibly have it. We disqualify ourselves due to a lack of faith in God. Refuse to remain a slave to fear and take a bold step into your destiny!

Sometimes if you don't see it, you can't achieve it. That is why the Bible says in Habakkuk 2:2, "And the LORD answered me, and said, 'Write the vision, and make it plain upon tables, that he may run that readeth it.'" It is important to write down the things that God has told you so that when they actualize, you will have evidence of the undeniable power of God's purpose in your life. It's time to make a move and write the vision.

Write five things that you enjoy doing, things that you do well:

1. _____
2. _____
3. _____
4. _____
5. _____

Write three vision statements for your life for the next six months:

1. _____
2. _____
3. _____

Write three vision statements for the next year:

1. _____
2. _____
3. _____

Chapter 9:
Use Your Toolbox

> Trust me. If you look really hard, you will find joy in your toolbox.
> —Dr. Cassandra Altenor

I remember talking to one of my dearest friends Cathy, about our children and how much we desire for them to serve God with their whole heart and also fear Him. After she mentioned to me some of her concerns about her son, the Holy Spirit just dropped something in my spirit. So, as I shared it with her, I will also share it with you.

We have all been provided a set of God-given tools in a toolbox—gifts and talents—to fulfill our destiny and for His glory. Most of the time, the devil tries to tempt us to look at everyone else's toolkit and dismiss the tools that God gave us. Which means we say to ourselves that we should be taller, slimmer, have more money, live in a different zip code, etc.

For example, there was a young man named King David in the Bible who loved God and was given a task to fight one of the biggest and fearful giants named Goliath. You have to understand when the enemy knows that God has a calling on your life the enemy will always send the spirit of intimidation against you to bring fear. You see, for forty days, Goliath and the enemies tormented the Israelites and tried to put fear in them. King Saul, the current king of Israelites was so fearful of David losing the battle because of his age and lack of experience in battle that he offered to give David his own armor, but David refused it because it wasn't his tool.

Often, we are tempted to operate in someone else's anointing, but God has called and anointed you for a specific task that only you can get done. If we would turn our energy and time to what God has given us, then we would be more joyful and more fulfilled. We have to understand that we don't necessarily have to worry about what everyone else is doing with their toolbox, but how we use ours. God knows what we can handle, and He has made provisions for our future. All we have to do is sharpen our tools so that when God opens an opportunity for us, we will be ready.

Find a Quiet Place
When you are thinking "How did I get here?" and you're in your low season, find some quiet place to meet with God. Your mind may be filled with doubt, fears, and lies from the enemy, but as I shared in earlier chapters, there is a place in God that will give you an inner peace that no one can give you. We often try to find other solutions, try to change careers, try to change our physical locations, but most of the time, we just need to run to God. The word of God says in Matthew 6:33, "But seek ye first the kingdom of God, and his righteousness; and all these things shall be added unto you." Often times, people think they don't have time or don't have the extra bedroom but finding a quiet place can be in your car during lunchtime or waking up early and meditating on the word of God. God just desires that we seek Him and pray!

You know what? It is in our quiet time that God speaks to us, just like Elijah. You have to be real with God if you truly want deliverance. Remember, you have to tell God the truth about how you are feeling, your fears, your thoughts, and what is in your heart because He knows exactly where you are, and He knows the level of pressure that you can handle. The word of God says in II Corinthians 12:9, "And he said unto me, my grace is sufficient for thee: for my strength is made perfect in weakness. Most gladly therefore will I rather glory in my infirmities, that the power of Christ may rest upon me."

The enemy will want you to forget the many times that God delivered you. Elijah nearly forgot the great event on Carmel Mountain. He said, "I am the only one left." God had to remind him that there were seven thousand people who loved him. Elijah asked the Lord to take away his life because the enemy Jezebel promised to kill him in the next twenty-four hours.

Similar to what Jezebel told Elijah, the enemy has told you a lie: you are loved by God and you are not alone. He said in His word that He will never leave nor forsake us. God wants to free your mind from the wrong concept and perception. God wants to replace your worry and fear with joy and peace. Just know that half of the things that we worry about 99.9% of the time never happen, so you might as well live in the fullness of joy that the Lord has given you.

The Power of a Prayer Life
Arthur W. Pink once said, "Prayer is the way and means God has appointed for the communication of the blessings of His goodness to His people."[47] I remember that one of the very first book I read becoming a Christian was called *The Attributes of God* by Arthur W. Pink was one of the very first Christian-author books that I read when I just got saved, and it was recommended by my Pastor. It was so good. It taught me about the attributes of God, which was

so crucial for me to learn because it helped me to understand who God is based on His attributes.

Starting your day with God and giving Him praise always will keep you grounded and connected to the Holy Spirit. Start your day in prayer with joy in God's presence. Matthew 6:6 states, "But thou, when thou prayest, enter into thy closet, and when thou hast shut thy door, pray to thy Father which is in secret; and thy Father which seeth in secret shall reward thee openly." You should have a place where you lay before God and talk to your Father daily. God doesn't want us to seek His face only when we are in trouble; we should seek Him daily. The word goes further in that same scripture in verses 11–12, "Give us this day our daily bread. And forgive us our debts, as we forgive our debtors." So, the word of God is our daily (spiritual) bread. We need God's word and a good prayer life to be a successful Christian.

The word says John 15:5, "I am the vine, ye are the branches: He that abideth in me, and I in him, the same bringeth forth much fruit: for without me ye can do nothing." Having a prayer life will keep us humble and connected to the Lord. God will never deny you access into His presence because He is our Abba father. The word of God says in Proverbs 8:17, "I love them that love me; and those that seek me early shall find me." Prayer is like a key that unlocks the door into the supernatural realm. Prayer also strengthens us in this journey called life.

When you have a prayer life, it allows joy to flow through your life. The word of God declares in John 7:38, "He that believeth on me, as the scripture hath said, out of his belly shall flow rivers of living water." All you have to do is believe in Jesus Christ, and the Holy Spirit will flow and reveal the mysteries of God through your prayer life. Prayer is one of the essential keys to being free from every spiritual chain that the enemy has bound you with. The presence of God is the place where we find peace and comfort.

Prayer brings us to a place where God can break and make us again. God desires us to be true to Him. The word of God says in Psalms 51:6, "Behold, thou desirest truth in inward parts: and in hidden part thou shalt make me to know wisdom." The psalmist David realized that through all his afflictions, betrayal, and enemies, heartaches, God wants the truth that is in our hearts.

Paul writes in First Thessalonians 5:16-18, "Rejoice always, pray without ceasing, and give thanks in all circumstances; for this is the will of God in Christ Jesus for you" (ESV). This is how God wants us to live: in joy, prayer, and thanksgiving; He wants us to live a life that is pleasing to God. "Rejoicing always" does not mean that we are to paste a fake smile on our faces, no matter what is going on in our lives or the lives of those we love. It means that we are to remain steadfast in our knowledge that God is our strength and comfort, no matter the circumstances we find ourselves in. If our relationship with Jesus is right, and we confess and repent our sins, we will experience this supernatural joy at all times whether those times are good or bad.

Don't allow circumstances to take away your joy. The word of God says in I Thessalonians 5:16–18 "Rejoice evermore. Pray without ceasing. In everything give thanks: for this is the will of God in Christ Jesus concerning you." When you start giving God thanks, you will soon realize how much joy that you will receive when you know that God can get you through anything that the enemy puts in your way, whether it is sickness, loss of a job, grief, heartache, fear, or anxiety—prayer and the blood of Jesus works.

> "Prayer is not so much an act as it is an attitude—
> an attitude of dependency, dependency upon God."
> —Arthur W. Pink

"The Christian soldier must avoid two evils—he must not faint or yield in the time of fight, and after a victory he must not wax insolent and secure. When he has overcome, he is to behave himself as though he were presently again to be assaulted. For Satan's temptations, like the waves of the sea, do follow one in the neck of the other."
—George Downame

"Real prayer is communion with God, so that there will be common thoughts between His mind and ours. What is needed is for Him to fill our hearts with His thoughts, and then His desires will become our desires flowing back to Him."
—Arthur W. Pink

Develop a Life of Selflessness

I learned that to receive something from God requires us to have self-denial and selflessness. The more you die to your own will, the more Christ lives through you. The second essential discipline you will need is a fasting life. I know a lot of people believe in The Daniel Fast. I don't have anything against that, but in my life, it was when I abstained from food completely that I got some of my greatest breakthroughs in the spiritual realm. But by acquiring a regular habit of denying behaviors, you get lower in His presence. And when you get lower in His presence, you are actually getting higher. Keep these scriptures in your heart:

> **Galatians 2:20:** I am crucified with Christ: nevertheless I live; yet not I, but Christ liveth in me: and the life which I now live in the flesh I live by the faith of the Son of God, who loved me and gave Himself for me.

Luke 9:23: And he said to them all, If any man will come after me, let him deny himself, and take up his cross daily, and follow me.

Galatians 5:24: And they that are Christ's have crucified the flesh with the affections and lusts.

Mark 8:35: For whosoever will save his life shall lose it; but whosoever shall lose his life for my sake and the gospel's, the same shall save it.

John 12:24: Verily, verily, I say unto you, except a corn of wheat fall into the ground and die, it abideth alone: but if it die, it bringeth forth much fruit.

Matthew 10:38: And he that taketh not his cross, and followeth after me, is not worthy of me.

Get Rid of the Spirit of Offense
We see the word "offend" appear twenty-five times. The Bible states that "A brother offended (pasha) is harder to be won than a strong city: and their contentions are like the bars of a castle" (Proverbs 18:19).

Get rid of the spirit of offense. Offense is a spirit whose primary job is to bring disunity in the body of Christ. It is a spirit that will try to entangle you and trap you from being in God's presence because the word of God says that to be carnally minded is death, not physical death, but to be spiritually minded is life and peace. You have to guard your heart against these demonic spirits that are assigned to steal your peace and joy. If you are easily offended when someone says something, you need to get rid of it. If you are easily saddened by what people say to you, you need to get rid of it. The enemy will tell you things like, "I'm right and they are wrong," but that is just the spirit of pride and self-righteousness, and it is not of God. This spirit tried to take a hold of my life, and I had to rebuke it because I realized that it was trying to rob my joy. After being sick and coming close to death, nothing else matters but God's presence.

We should not focus on the little things. Look at the big picture and the real assignment that God has for our life. The spirit of offense will come with his cousins called hatred, malice, jealousy, and many other evil spirits. The spirit of offense is of the devil and it causes us not to have the true love of God for others in our hearts, and it will eventually steal our joy. Don't let the ugliness of others' behavior kill the beauty and treasure that God has placed in you. Don't let the spirit of offense rule your emotions and steal your joy.

Strengthen the Power of Endurance
The power of endurance is to stand firm under the pressure of life. The word endurance means "the power to withstand pain or hardships; the ability or strength to continue despite being fatigued, stressed, or other adverse conditions with courage." It's been said that two things can define you: your patience when you have nothing and your attitude when you have everything. When you are going through your hardest times, God will reveal Himself to you as your peace. You have to know Him. You can't read about Him—you need to experience Him in His glory. God must be revealed to you through His word and glory. Some of my favorite scriptures are the following verses from Romans 5:1–6:

1: Therefore, being justified by faith, we have peace with God through our Lord Jesus Christ:
2: By whom also we have access by faith into this grace wherein we stand and rejoice in hope of the glory of God.

3: And not only so, but we glory in tribulations also: knowing that tribulation worketh patience;
4: And patience, experience; and experience, hope:
5: And hope maketh not ashamed; because the love of God is shed abroad in our hearts by the Holy Ghost which is given unto us.
6: For when we were yet without strength, in due time Christ died for the ungodly.

When tough times come, use your faith to stand through your season of adversity. You see, in the book of Job, it was God that asked the enemy this question: "Have you considered my servant, Job?" Although Job was one of the wealthiest men of his time, there came a time when his money couldn't help keeping him from experiencing loss. You see, it was under the Lord's sovereign providence that Satan was allowed to frustrate Job's purpose. Job had lost it all; he lost his children, servants, property, and fortune, and his wife was no help. But all during this period of loss, Job's faith never wavered. He blessed the name of God, acknowledging that the Lord is ultimately in control. One of the most significant parts in the book of Job is when he maintained his integrity. In Job 2:9, his wife said to him, "Are you still maintaining your integrity? Curse God and die!" It is important to maintain good integrity, which simply means you hold on to what you believe in your core.

Speak Life & Self-Affirmations
Toby Mac is a Christian songwriter and singer who stated, "God is still writing your story. Quit trying to steal the pen."

Your words have power. They are like a hammer; they can build, and they can also tear down. We need to stop making defeated statements over our lives. We need to speak healing words from the word of God. Proverbs 18:21 says, "Death and life are in the power of the tongue: and they that love it shall eat the fruit thereof." Speaking into your atmosphere the word of God and saying some self-affirmations will help bring back your joy. Here are some of the things we may tell ourselves when we've lost our joy:

1. I am a nobody.
2. I am insignificant.
3. I can never be that (or achieve that, or finish that).
4. I am the worst person in my family.

Cancel those lies and replace them with the word of God through these thirty affirmations:

1. I am the righteousness of God.
2. I am anointed.
3. I am healed.
4. I am favored.
5. I am powerful in Christ.
6. I am victorious and an overcomer.
7. I am that apple of His eye.
8. He teaches my hands to war and my fingers to fight.
9. I am that I am created me.
10. I was created in the image of our God.
11. Weeping may endure for a night but joy cometh in the morning.
12. I am the head and not the tail.
13. I will be strong and do exploits.
14. I am good enough, strong enough, smart enough, brave enough, and attractive enough.

15. I believe in the God that created me with everything I need to succeed in life, with nothing lacking and nothing missing. I shall be made whole, physically, emotionally, spiritually, and financially.
16. I am intelligent, confident, and capable of doing this job, raising this family, serving in this ministry, etc.
17. I see each setback as a set up to my new season.
18. I fortify the walls of my mind and I reject every lie of the enemy.
19. I knowingly uproot every negative seed that has been planted in my mind.
20. I send it back to the sender every negative word or action that has been said in my life.
21. I arrest and dismantle every spiritual suicide that the enemy has attempted on my life.
22. I veto and nullify every sabotage and network that gathers to steal my joy.
23. I revoke the spirit of oppression and depression that has been assigned to destroy my life.
24. I dismantle every spirit of condemnation and every self-inflicting wound that has allowed me to be stagnant in my walk with Christ.
25. I am free from every negative thought and influence of my past through the blood of Jesus.
26. I call for the spirit of joy to overflow in my life by the power of the Holy Ghost.
27. I accept that I am blessed and have found favor in the sight of the Lord.
28. I am Fruitful.
29. I am Forgiving.
30. I am Thankful.

You must bind every antagonizing bully that has attacked your life and has tried to stop you from fulfilling your destiny. The anointing will destroy every yoke of bondage in your life. Forbid the enemy from taking your joy; you are not hopeless. Don't give him your joy, but fight for it. You deserve it, and Jesus Christ already paid through His precious blood for it.

God Will Provide Someone to Encourage You
God tells us that we are never alone because He is always with us. However, He recognizes when we need some assistance from someone on Earth. In your valley season, God will always provide a way for us to receive the encouragement that we need to go on. God uses people in our lives to bless us. In the book of Kings chapter 19, we find that Elijah is entering into a season of deep depression. Although God used him to accomplish many marvelous victories, because of the threat of him losing his life, he runs away to hide. He finds himself resting under a juniper tree. Elijah then prays to God and ask God to take his life because of fear, but God knowing that He had a bigger plan and assignment for Elijah, he gave him grace to go on. Often times we are at our last end, but God has a way of re-fueling our souls and giving us the grace to go on.

God knew that Elijah needed that support; God shows His love to us through the people He sends in our lives. God will never leave you in the hands of the enemy, but He will always make a way of escape and will bring you deliverance. You see, in II Kings 3:11, "But Jehosophat said, 'Is there not here a prophet of the Lord, that we may enquire of the Lord by him?' And one of the kings of Israel's servants answered and said, "Here is Elisha the son of Shaphat, which poured water on the hands of Elijah.'"

I have a beautiful friend who is truly a gift from God, and her name is Cathy—better known as my sister who has many times in my down days poured out water on my hands. The way we met is so funny. I was in college and taking this difficult calculus course. I used to commute to school downtown, which hardly had parking and I also couldn't afford the monthly parking pass, so I would be late to practically all my classes. Classes had started and I registered late, and I came to the class two days after it had already started. I turned around and asked Cathy, "Hey, can I see your notes?"

She had this look on her face like "The nerve of you," but I am not one who takes no for an answer. At first, she seemed like she was ignoring me, and then I asked again. I know she gave it to me because she felt bad, after which we just started studying together. We started to meet to study and I started to share my faith with her. I then found out that she had a relationship with the Lord when she was young, so I just kept praying that God would touch her, and He did. We have been friends ever since.

She has been there for me in some of my darkest times, and has encouraged me, so I pray that God will provide you with someone that will be heaven-sent, someone that will pour out the love of God on you and will encourage you in your dark season, with no hidden agenda, no ulterior motive, but just the pure love of Jesus. I believe that God gives us these words to show us that if He could do it for Elijah, Jeremiah, Ruth, David, and many others in the Bible that were discouraged, He can do it for us. The word of God says in Romans 15:4, "For whatsoever things were written aforetime were written for our learning, that we through patience and comfort of the scriptures might have hope." His word brings us joy and hope. If people leave you or walk out of your life, let them go because God will provide you with someone who is going to be your side, and will pour out love on you.

Joy attracts joy, peace attracts peace, complaints attract complainers, and gossip attracts gossipers, so you must watch who is in your inner circle, and if they are joyful or not. I remember very early on in my Christian walk, God removed people that truly weren't going where he was taking me. Slowly but surely, I was rejected by most group outings and stopped hanging out with a certain group of people because God knew that these people weren't following Christ like I was pursuing Him. I didn't understand it, until I started understanding my calling. I Corinthians 15:33 states, "Be not deceived: evil communications corrupt good manners." This means that when you start hanging around someone who is negative or someone who has a faulty character, eventually, you will begin to speak like that person and behave like them also. The other scripture that I love is James 3:11, KJV: "Doth a fountain send forth at the same place sweet *water* and bitter?" You cannot have good and bad stuff coming out of the same place. This includes your thoughts, your mind, and your company.

I'm Living My Best Life in Christ!
There is a quote I read by Bill Keane, a famous cartoonist, who said, "Yesterday is history, tomorrow is a mystery, today is a gift of God, which is why we call it the present."[48] You will never be able to go back into the past and change what happened, but you are not a victim of your past nor your circumstance—you are a winner through Jesus Christ. Refuse to allow your past to sabotage your future. I have heard from my beloved pastor and I believe this statement: "My worst day in Christ is better than my best day without Him because not having God in your life even if it looks like you're doing good, you are still losing; because the enemy is out to kill your future." God has a wonderful plan for your life. Jeremiah 29:11 says, "For I know the thoughts that I think toward you, saith the Lord, thoughts of peace, and not of evil, to give you an expected end." It is so good to know that the

God of the universe is thinking about you and me. You really have nothing to worry about—God's got this!

You've got now, you don't have yesterday, and only God knows about tomorrow, so don't allow anxiety and fear to cripple your life. Half the things that we worry about will never happen; you are just wasting your energy and precious time. Your joy and peace of mind are worth fighting for.

I have learned that having enemies will always keep us humble and dependent on God and not on our strengths. When I was young in faith, I was sad when I didn't have people's approval. This used to frustrate me until I changed. I started believing who God said I was. My perspective of why opposition is truly necessary for us to be processed. Indeed, adversities are not designed to kill us but to strengthen our faith.

For example, King David in the Bible was anointed at a young age of seventeen years old and prophesized over him such a great future. David's destiny was revealed at a young age when he was anointed by the prophet Samuel in front of his brothers. David's own father didn't support him or considered him when the prophet Samuel came searching for who God wanted him to anoint. David had countless internal oppositions such as his family. He had to deal with rape, murder, and conspiracy in his family, and also external issues like this leader King Saul. He had so many dysfunctional things going on, but God favored him. God was sovereign to David because he had a heart toward God.

Adversity and oppositions are used to fuel our prayer and fasting life. II Corinthians 4:8–9 says, "We are hard pressed on every side, but not crushed; perplexed, but not in despair; persecuted, but not abandoned; struck down, but not destroyed." God will not allow the enemy to destroy your life. The Lord always delivered David from his enemies. The word of God says in I Peter 5:10, "And the God of all grace, who called you to his eternal glory in Christ, after you have suffered a little while, will Himself restore you and make you strong, firm and steadfast."

I am so grateful to be alive, that I refuse to not have joy and peace of mind. My joy is non-negotiable, it's mine because Jesus died on the cross so I could have joy.

"God sweetens outward pain with inward peace."
—Thomas Watson

"Afflictions are light when compared with what we really deserve. They are light when compared with the sufferings of the Lord Jesus. But perhaps their real lightness is best seen by comparing them with the weight of glory which is awaiting us."
—Arthur W. Pink

Never Give up Hope
"Never give up. Have hope.
Expect only the best from life and take action to get it."
—Catherine Pulsifer

The famous biblical scholar Charles Spurgeon said, "Do not bury a man before he is dead; hope that so long as a sinner lives, he may yet live unto God." My desire is for God's children to know their entitlement and be free from the bondage and plans of the devil. That you may have the joy of the Lord in your hearts. There is no issue or condition that God cannot fix and make you brand new.

I believe that as long as a person has breath, they have hope—hope for salvation and hope for deliverance. You have to learn how to persevere in life. My mom is one of my inspirations when it comes to perseverance. When my father walked out of our lives, she became a single mother of three girls overnight. She had never worked because she was a stay-at-home mom. She never complained nor panicked; she just kept things going and moving. She was resilient and she made sure that we had a roof over our head and food on our table. She taught me courage and strength.

You have to be persistent about keeping your joy. Every day you wake up, you must give God thanks for a new day and declare that it will be filled with joy and peace. One of my favorite scriptures is Joel 2:32: "And it shall come to pass, that whosoever shall call on the name of the Lord shall be delivered: for in mount Zion and in Jerusalem shall be deliverance, as the Lord hath said, and in the remnant whom the Lord shall call." This scripture gives me hope that no matter what I am facing, all I have to do is cry out to God for my deliverance. There were so many nights that I cried out to God with my pillows filled with tears of sorrow, and He has never left me nor forsake me. He is just waiting for you to cry out to Him.

Let Praise Be Your Weapon!
There has never been a time in my life when I gave God praise and He didn't come through for me. There will be moments when you will be facing the storms of life and you will feel discouraged and oppressed, but you still have to praise God because praising God is not a feeling; it's a relationship. Psalms 103:1 says, "Bless the Lord, O my soul: and all that is within me, bless his holy name."

You have to learn how to praise God till you go through and get on the other side of your Jordan. The Israelites had to cross Jordan. They had so many issues keeping them from crossing over, but God was bigger than any sea, and so is He today. He is bigger than the problem or battle that you will encounter in life. Walter Cradock said, "Take a saint, and put him into any condition, and he knows how to rejoice in the Lord."

When you rejoice, you are confusing the enemy because his intention is to steal, to kill, and to destroy your life is intercepted in the spiritual realm. But when he can't kill you, he attempts to steal your family, your health, your peace, and your joy. I love these quotes because they encourage and strengthen my journey.

> A truly humble man is sensible of his natural distance from God; of his dependence on Him; of the insufficiency of his own power and wisdom; and that it is by God's power that he is upheld and provided for, and that he needs God's wisdom to lead and guide him, and His might to enable him to do what he ought to do for Him.
> —Jonathan Edwards

> Believers have joy and comfort—that joy that angels cannot give, and devils cannot take.
> —Christopher Fowler

> Christ ceaseth not to work by His intercession with God for us, and by His Spirit in us for God, whereby He upholds His saints, their graces, their comforts in life, without which they would run to ruin.
> —William Gurnall

> Your life is short, your duties many, your assistance great, and your reward sure; therefore, faint not, hold on and hold up, in ways of well-doing, and heaven shall make amends for all
> —Thomas Brooks

Self-Care Tips of Joy Maintenance

Every day ask God to help you be the best version of yourself and share that with the world. Be authentic to who God made you to be. Here are acts of self-care for maintaining your joy.

First, it helps to be able to laugh. This life is filled with hardship, disappointment, heartbreak, and sorrow. A good laugh will recharge your battery. The word of God says that laughter is medicine. Proverbs 17:22 says, "A merry heart doeth good like a medicine: but a broken spirit drieth the bones." This is saying that a happy heart is just like taking some good medicine. Laughter is able to cure a multitude of diseases. When you are able to laugh, laugh a lot and laugh hard. Surround yourself with people that make you laugh, people who don't take life too seriously. I say this because there is a person right now in the doctor's office about to find out that they have cancer, a chronic disease, or they are about to get some other form of bad news, but our hope is in God.

There is not another you in this world, so you must invest in your spiritual walk and your emotional, physical, and mental needs. Take care of yourself. If you don't, you will have nothing to give to others. I had to learn after spending a month in the hospital that I have to do better in taking care of myself. Here are thirty things that you can do for self-care:

1. Make a daily affirmation of who you are in God. Love yourself enough and speak life.
2. Start a journal.
3. Create a vision board.
4. Join a gym.
5. Go on long walks.
6. Meditate on the word of God.
7. Write down what you are grateful for.
8. Pamper yourself and go to a spa.
9. Get rid of junk and clutter in your life.
10. Get rid of toxic people in your life.
11. Breathe deeply.
12. Buy yourself some flowers (one of my favorite things to do).
13. Make a lunch date with an old friend.

14. Write yourself a love letter.
15. Find a reason to laugh.
16. Admire yourself in the mirror.
17. Keep your thoughts clean and pure.
18. Do something creative.
19. Start planting a garden.
20. Find a hobby.
21. Dance like crazy.
22. Smile a lot.
23. Get plenty of sleep and go to bed on time.
24. Offer a random act of kindness.
25. Go to a nursing home or spend time with your grandparents and gain some wisdom.
26. Write a list of everything that brings you joy.
27. Seek divine connections and not validation.
28. Slow down, be present, and don't rush life.
29. Unplug from technology.
30. Make a list of at least thirty things that you love about yourself.

Please note there are so many more things, but these are just my top thirty. I pray that you will move forward with the fullness of joy that God has given His children and His abundance of grace.

Make a list of changes that you need to make to improve self-care.

1._____
2._____
3._____
4._____
5._____

Chapter 10: Jesus Will Give You Beauty for Your Ashes

Life is not easy.

We all have faced (or will face) some challenging events. There are difficulties that even the strongest person may not be able to handle. Sometimes we feel overwhelmed, and fear comes upon us. We may be feeling frustrated and weary.

But we can have peace in knowing that Jesus Christ loves us so much that he came and died for all our rejections, traumas, disappointments, and ups and downs that He knew that we would be facing through life. Only the power of God is able to keep and sustain us through these difficult seasons. Just know that your anchor has to be in Christ because everything else is bound to fail.

Waiting on God requires hope, faith, and patience. It is not an easy task to wait, but if we do wait and trust God through the process, we will reap all the wonderful benefits and rewards. The word of God says in Isaiah 40:31, "But they that wait upon the Lord shall renew their strength; they shall mount up with wings as eagles; they shall run, and not be weary; and they shall walk, and not faint."

The verse starts with a few powerful words. "But they that wait." You see the Hebrew word 'wait' also means, "hope for' and 'anticipate." You can't afford to lose your hope in God. Trust me, you may lose some relationships, you may lose your job or house, but do not lose your hope.

The world that we are currently living in is filled with uncertainty of tomorrow. We find the few people who are loyal. Things are moving fast and changing all the time, so we must know that Jesus Christ is our hope. You may be wondering, "So what does it mean to have hope?"

[49]*Hope* in Hebrew actually means "to expect" or have some sort of expectation.

1. A desire of some good, accompanied with at least a slight expectation of obtaining it, or a belief that it is obtainable. Hope differs from wish and desire in this, that it implies some expectation of obtaining the good desired, or the possibility of possessing it. Hope therefore always gives pleasure or joy; whereas wish and desire may produce or be accompanied with pain and anxiety.

2. Confidence in a future event; the highest degree of well-founded expectation of good; as a hope founded on God's gracious promises; a scriptural sense.

4. An opinion or belief not amounting to certainty but grounded on substantial evidence. To cherish a desire of food, with some expectation of obtaining it, or a belief that it is obtainable.

To place confidence in; to trust in with confident expectation of good.

Why art thou cast down, O my soul, and why art thou disquieted within me? Hope thou in God. Ps.43.

[50]HOPE, v.t. To desire with expectation of good, or a belief that it may be obtained. But as a transitive verb, it is seldom used, and the phrases in which it is so used are elliptical, for being understood.

A great example of hope is found in Genesis chapter fifteen, where God made a covenant with Abram. He cried out to God and began to complain to God about not having any offspring to call heir. God responds to Abram with a promise. [51]"I will give you a son by her. I will bless her, and she shall become nations; kings of peoples shall come from her" (Genesis 15:16). Abram responds, "Shall a child be born to a man who is a hundred years old? Shall Sarah, who is ninety years old, bear a child?" (Genesis 15:17).

God promises Abram that he will have a son of his own and Abram, the word said in Romans 4:3 "believed the Lord and he counted it to him as righteousness." When you are waiting on God for two or three months, that is not bad. Even if you're waiting on God for a few years, your hope doesn't shift.

So, at this point, Abram believed the Lord and didn't question God; he still had hope. But Abram looked at his wife's old age and physical conditions. This seemed impossible for God to handle.

Countless times, I hear people say God has promised them to heal, deliverance, a husband, a baby, a wife, a child, or a home. Everything around you may look like it is not going to happen, but you have to activate your faith. The word of God says in Hebrews 11:1 "Now faith is the substance of things hoped for, the evidence of things not seen," which means that although you don't physically see it, you believe what God said about that situation. As long as you stay faithful, humble, and committed to God, He will always come through for you.

I was laying sick from food poisoning in the hospital for three weeks. Although my family loved me, and my Pastor, church family came and visited me, I knew my hope and my faith in Christ was all I had. I was so sick that sometimes I didn't even realize that they were there. When I was aware, they were there, I was so grateful for their presence, and although they came, they had to go. But God was right there with me. I felt God's presence in that room. He was my Comforter and my Healer. This is why I am so unapologetic about my love for Jesus and my faith in Him. God has been there for me in some of my darkest times, and He will be there for you.

During my stay at the hospital, around two o'clock in the morning every night for four straight nights the voice of the enemy was constantly waking me up. This evil force would literally wake me up and say, "You are not going to make it. I am going to kill you." Every night, I would just sit up on that hospital bed and confess Psalms 118:17: "I shall not die, but live, and declare the works of the Lord." I would repeat it over and over until I fell asleep. I couldn't call anybody at those hours, but that was okay because all I had to do was call out to Jesus and I felt God push back the powers of darkness.

By the time I left the hospital, I was so happy to be back home because you see I was going through a rough time. I remember one day I was so low in my spirit and my dear Sis Stacy stopped by and to see me but she surprised me and brought her make-up, and she is a phenomenal hair dresser and she brought all her tools and fixed my hair and gave me a make over right on the hospital bed. You see that might mean much to me, but if you know me I love to do my make up and my hair, I love being a lady, so she was in tune with who I was and God spoke to her to do that for me because he knew how low I was. She was patient, gentle and kind and that is what I needed, just to feel myself again. God is just so amazing, He will put people in your life that will bless you in a way that will leave you speechless. I felt the tears flowing down my chin because I said to myself, you sent Sis Stacy as my little angel so I would stay in a state of depression. God also provided many different people to come and encourage me during this time and I am so grateful. I attended Wednesday night Bible studies. Around one o'clock in the morning, I felt like a truck was on top of my chest and I couldn't breathe. I called for the ambulance. Every second felt like a day, I was in so much pain. I couldn't walk to the ambulance. I just collapsed. I spent another two weeks in the hospital, and I had to fight all types of psychological warfare, but I thank God for some wonderful brothers and sisters that He blessed me with during this season like my Pastor, Sis Thompson, Deacon Warren and his wife, Sis Jay, Sis Candy (who is so selfless and a blessing to God's kingdom), Cathy, Sis Kimmie, Sis Asia, Sis Marie, Sis Neva, Sis Keisha, Sis Patsey, Sis Sheare and Bro Mulique, Bro Sefan, and all the leaders at my church, to name a few who came and spent time and encouraged me in the hospital. Some couldn't come but they called, and I was grateful for that too. I thank God for also for my immediate family, aunts and cousins who also was there. Just know that no matter what battle you are facing God will always surround you with His love through others. I love and thank God for my church family. The battle was intense, but the Lord delivered me, and I am so grateful for the cross, His word, and His blood.

While you are waiting on God for a promise, you have to encourage yourself through the word of God. When you are discouraged, tired, and frustrated, just remember to hope in God. You see, Abraham and Sarah waited twenty-five years on God for a promise. No matter how long it may take, you have to wait on God for your promise.

God has proven Himself to be faithful over and over again in my life. During my hardships, I realized that we are nothing but clay. I am absolutely nothing without God breathing on me. When I reached the hospital, I was shocked to hear that I had pneumonia. The enemy wanted me to lose my hope. I was so down at one point and I had to encourage myself in the word of God.

For some of you, right now, the enemy is trying to do the same thing to you. But don't lose your hope in Jesus Christ. When you are feeling discouraged, here is one of my favorite scriptures, Psalms 42:11:

> Why art thou cast down, O my soul? and why art thou disquieted within me? hope thou in God: for I shall yet praise him, who is the health of my countenance, and my God.

The Grace to Go On
God is the one who gives us the grace to go on. I couldn't understand and was so frustrated, but the Holy Spirit revealed to me that God had a greater purpose in this season. The enemy wants us to lose our hope and joy in Jesus Christ. We have to trust God, knowing that He is able to deliver His children from all storms of life. He wants you to create your own backup plan, but you have to have faith.

My Pastor always tells us that "a faith that is not tested is not a faith that is worth having." Sarah was deceived and could no longer wait on God's promise. So, she decided to take matters into her own hands and felt that she could help God hasten the process.

I love to watch the infomercial that talks about if you take this pill, you will burn five thousand calories and lose three hundred pounds. Half the time, it's a high dosage of caffeine that gives you energy, producing an extreme high, but then you experience extreme lows. They are very bad for your health, and once you stop taking them, you gain all the weight back (trust me, I've taken a few).

You see, these are called shortcuts, and when we are waiting on God, the enemy always creates these shortcuts for us so we could give up on God's promise. Abram, instead of waiting on God's perfect will, followed Sarah's advice and slept with his maid, Hagar, which wasn't God's original plan. You can't afford to faint while you are waiting on God. You will have those moments when you are discouraged. Don't settle for the devil's junk. It may look good today but will bring much heartache tomorrow. Just wait for God and His divine timing, His perfect gift, and His promise for you. Abraham had to wait twenty-five years for his promise, and this is why the word of the Lord says:

Isaiah 40:31: But they that wait upon the Lord shall renew their strength; they shall mount up with wings as eagles; they shall run, and not be weary; and they shall walk, and not faint.

Psalms 121:7-8: The Lord shall preserve thee from all evil: he shall preserve thy soul. The Lord shall preserve thy going out and thy coming in from this time forth, and even for evermore.

Romans 15:13: Now the God of hope fill you with all joy and peace in believing, that ye may abound in hope, through the power of the Holy Ghost.

Psalm 31:24: Be of good courage, and he shall strengthen your heart, all ye that hope in the Lord.

Lamentation 3:24: The Lord is my portion, saith my soul; therefore will I hope in him.

I Peter 1:3: Blessed be the God and Father of our Lord Jesus Christ, which according to his abundant mercy hath begotten us again unto a lively hope by the resurrection of Jesus Christ from the dead.

The Enemy Wants You to Lose Hope

The enemy wants you to *lose hope*. He wants you to stop working, praying, and caring. The enemy's goal is to stop you from being an instrumental part of the Kingdom of God, and he does this by killing your hope. Keep hope alive knowing that "The Lord will withhold no good thing from those who do what is right" (Psalm 84:11).

Maybe you have been praying to God about a job or seeking him for a new direction. Some of you are young and single and asking God to send you a mate that loves God and loves you for who Christ called you to be. Maybe you are in the hospital or have someone you love that is going through a really rough season in life and wondering where God is.

One of my favorite people in the world, affectionately named 'Aunt Roro" passed away from a tragic car accident in which she was talking to me in the back seat of the car on her way to church when a young man talking on the phone ran into the car that she was in and she died. Knowing that I was the last person she spoke to, know that I loved her so much, and my youngest sister passing away at the age of twenty-five, I was constantly asking God, "Why? What is happening?" One of the darkest seasons that I had to face, and God gave me grace during this season. It was easy to get frustrated and lose hope. I am still here, believing in God for my healing. Some days I wake up with so much pain, but I have faith that my God is going to deliver me from this. God is working on your behalf too.

The Potter's Wheel
In Christian art, the eagle often represents the resurrection of Christ because the sight of an eagle rising in flight is powerful. To have one's youth renewed like the eagle is metaphorically to be "renewed," restored to our original state of perfection and strength in the Lord before mankind sinned. God created mankind in His own image. The Hebrew word translated as "youth" means "early life." The "early life" of mankind is the life before sin. Going through a very dark time in my life when I experience grief, loss, and sickness, I had to plug into God, who sustained me and gave me the grace that I needed to get me through that rough time. God will keep you in your toughest moments and comfort you in your darkest times. He will also send a word to you in dew season. When I was so sick and was going in and out of the hospital and Bishop Carter who lives in Jamaica called my Pastor and said that God showed him that I was sick, and God also showed him me being like a salmon swimming up and going up. That was God encouraging me that That was God encouraging me that better days were coming, God lifted me up and delivered me from the spirit of infirmity (sickness). I thank God for spiritual fathers and mothers in my life like my Pastor and Bishop Carter. I held on to that word and knew that I was going to be okay, God was there with me.

During your waiting period, God will put you on what is called the potter's wheel. In Jeremiah 18, God shows us how he told his prophet to go to the potter's house to express to us that he is the potter, and we are the clay. I read a commentary that said "Like Jeremiah's clay pot, each of us will face one of two futures. Either we'll be shattered in the antitypical Valley of Hinnom, or we will be perfect vessels, gathered for use in God's House—either eternal destruction or eternal service" (Mal. 4:1; John 14:2, 3). God, our potter, will soon complete His constructive work in us. God is using our time as we wait to teach us several necessary life lessons.

The other lesson we need to learn is that we are not yet pots we are still clay in God's hands. He has the authority to mold us and make us into whomever He wants us to be. God, who is our potter, still works with us, on us, and in us, molding and forming "as seems good to Him" (Jer. 18:4). Allow the Holy Spirit to take you through the process.

The final lesson to learn is that if we are going to be used by God to do His kingdom work, we must pass through the fire. Don't stop when you are feeling the heat. Just keep walking through it and God will see you through. Life is filled with fiery trials—loss of a job, loss of a loved one—but we have hope in Jesus. Again, the enemy tells us all sorts of lies during this time to confuse us and make us lose hope.

His Divine Timing Is Amazing
The devil tells us that God is not going to come through, that He won't keep his promises, but God's divine timing is amazing. The same thing happened to Sarah when God gave her a promise. We give up too easily. We give up on our dreams, our marriages, our children, our friendships, our dreams, and our hope. Instead, we need to fight the enemy against every invasion. Our dreams are worth fighting for! Nehemiah stated in 4:14, "After I looked things over, I stood up and said to the nobles, the officials, and the rest of the people, 'Don't be afraid of them. Remember the Lord, who is great and awesome, and fight for your families, your sons and your daughters, your wives, and your homes.'"

Don't be afraid of those demonic forces that are ripping through your relationship and disturbing your peace. The enemy wants to remove and destroy everything in our lives that will bring us joy and give us peace. Our God is faithful and true to His promises. And always know that His grace is sufficient—His grace is all that you need. When you wait on God, you get inner peace, and you gain confidence in your God, knowing that He ultimately knows what is best for you, and He knows exactly where you are emotionally, and spiritually.

God Always Keeps His Promises
You will go through a time when it seems as if the dream and the vision that God gave you seems impossible. That is when you need faith. Confess this verse in Numbers 23:19: "God is not a man, that he should lie; neither the son of man, that he should repent: hath he said, and shall he not do it? or hath he spoken, and shall he not make it good?" God is not like humans, who love you today and hate you tomorrow; He is not going to manipulate you nor hurt you. You are safe in His arms. God always keeps His promises—the end!

I had some moments of despair where I would say, "Maybe, God, this is all in my mind. Maybe this is not your will for my life." I remember there was a time in my life where it seemed as if I was getting these countless prophecies. I remember once during our church convention, I used to help serve upstairs in our kitchen. A man of God said for someone to call me from upstairs, and he said, "Where is that young lady that was sitting here?" then he described what I was wearing and they sent for me, and he prophesized that God is going to use me for His kingdom, and this was happening frequently. I got a prophecy once that I would be speaking all over the world at conferences. These are a few of many that have not yet been manifested in my life, but I trust God that they will come to pass.

My dear sister in the Lord, Missionary Smith, always tells me "Cassie, leave it to time," And I thank her for those words of wisdom. I've learned that time heals the deepest wounds, and can erase painful memories and heartaches, but it is only through the power of the Holy Spirit that we can truly be healed. I would go to services and the Lord would just use the servant of God to call me and speak into my life. There was a disconnect with the prophecy and the manifestation, but I did the work. I poured my heart into the work of the kingdom. I got joy from serving people and I went to Bible school. Once again there is purpose in the process, and you must always be in Faith mode.

I was still waiting. But, as I was waiting, I decided to prepare myself for where God would be taking me. You see, you can't wait to get there and get ready—you have to *be* ready! Find out what is the will of God for your life and take a plow and start plowing. The word of God says, "Faith without works is dead."

A wonderful, lovely Pastor Millie visited our church during our Annual Convention. I love her spirit. She said in her message one year that we, as God's children, we have to "work the Word." Yes, every word of promise that is in the Bible belongs to God's children.

In the waiting process, the enemy will try to get you to jump ship, to quit, to give up, and to surrender, but you have to hold on to hope and the promises of God. Don't be impatient. Sometimes, we think that we are so ready, and God is saying, "If I don't get your mind fortified with my word, if I don't allow you to go through some ridicules, some disappointments, you will not be ready for the next phase in your life." You will go through a season where you feel that you have no support from anybody, but God is just processing you. He is your ultimate source that you seek help from. God alone. Ask God to help you to enjoy and rejoice in the task that is in front of you. Live in your present, and not so much in your future and definitely not in your past.

The enemy will also allow you to think that everyone's vision seems to be coming true, but you feel like you are on hold. I believe that most of the time when our expectations aren't met, we tend to lose hope and end up in a place of depression. Some scriptures to know:

Psalms 121:7-8: The Lord shall preserve thee from all evil: he shall preserve thy soul. The Lord shall preserve thy going out and thy coming in from this time forth, and even for evermore.

Romans 15:13: Now the God of hope fill you with all joy and peace in believing, that ye may abound in hope, through the power of the Holy Ghost.

Psalm 31:24: Be of good courage, and he shall strengthen your heart, all ye that hope in the Lord.

Lamentation 3:24: The Lord is my portion, saith my soul; therefore, will I hope in him.

I Peter 1:3: Blessed be the God and Father of our Lord Jesus Christ, which according to his abundant mercy hath begotten us again unto a lively hope by the resurrection of Jesus Christ from the dead.

Ephesians 4:4: There is one body, and one Spirit, even as ye are called in one hope of your calling.

God has called you before the foundation of this world for purpose and destiny. Yet, the enemy too knows your potential. But not to worry. You don't have to be scared of him because he is already defeated.

Ask for Your Grace
While you are waiting on God for your breakthrough and promise, you have to pray and ask God for His grace.

You see, accepting God's grace was difficult for me. I had to ask God to touch my mind and heal me from my past. I had to learn who God said that I was through His word and I had to change the way I thought. I always thought that no one would really love me if they knew my past, my shame, or my guilt, or the lies that I spent my entire youth telling myself that I was happy.

Also, this concept of grace was hard for me to accept and receive because although I felt the power of the presence of God, when I was by myself, I felt that perhaps I have to work really hard on being good. I didn't want to lose that feeling of being in God's presence. I was ashamed because I knew the lifestyle that He saved me from, and the enemy did his best job in reminding me constantly of how unworthy I was of His grace.

To help me to pray for His grace, I had to memorize the scripture that says Ephesians 2:8–9, "For by grace are ye saved through faith; and that not of yourselves: it is the gift of God: Not of works, lest any man should boast." In other words, there is no amount of money or physical labor that we could ever do for God to love us more nor less. He could never love us less, but His love is everlasting. You have to have a way to see your circumstances and yourself. Whatever has you contemplating negative thoughts, negative behavior, or addictive behaviors, look to the word of God for help. So, what is grace?

Grace is a constant theme in the Bible, and it culminates in the New Testament with the coming of Jesus (John 1:17). [52]The word translated "grace" in the New Testament comes from the Greek word *charis*, which means "favor, blessing, or kindness." We can all extend grace to others; but when the word grace is used in connection with God, it takes on a more powerful meaning. Grace is God choosing to bless us rather than curse us as our sin deserves. It is His benevolence to the undeserving.

According to Strong's dictionary, the word "grace" literally means "favor." In Hebrew it is *chen* from a root word *chanan*, to bend or stoop in kindness to another as a superior to an inferior. [53]In Greek, it is *charis* and has the idea of graciousness in manner or action. It comes from a root word *chairo* to be cheerful or happy. When used in reference to God, it is the benevolent action of Him stooping down to us in His kindness to reach us in our need and convey upon us a benefit. His grace has been termed "unmerited favor," but it is more than an attitude of favor or mercy. His mercy is an expression of His compassion toward us, but His grace is an extension of benevolence translated into action that releases His enabling power into our lives.

It is the unmerited favor, mercy, compassion, the undeserved blessing, a gift, God's loving mercy towards, mankind.

> "... who has saved us and called us with a holy calling, not according to our works, but according to His own purpose and grace which was given to us in Christ Jesus before time began." (2 Timothy 1:9).

"And if by grace, then it is no longer of works; otherwise, grace is no longer grace. But if it is of works, it is no longer grace; otherwise, work is no longer work." (Romans 11:6)

"Therefore, having been justified by faith, we have peace with God through our Lord Jesus Christ, through whom also we have access by faith into this grace in which we stand, and rejoice in hope of the glory of God." (Romans 5:1-2)

"For the grace of God that brings salvation has appeared to all men ..." (Titus 2:11)

"But we believe that through the grace of the Lord Jesus Christ we shall be saved in the same manner as they." (Acts 15:11)

"Grace is free sovereign favor to the ill-deserving." (**B.B. Warfield**)

"Grace is love that cares and stoops and rescues." (**John Stott**)

"Grace is the opposite of karma, which is all about getting what you deserve. Grace is getting what you don't deserve." (**Justin Holcomb**)

Nothing Can Separate Us from the Love of God

No amount of work—no matter how good and holy we think those works may be—will ever be good enough to get us back in the good graces of our Lord and Savior. Ritualism, legalism, and works are out the door! God will love you no matter what you do. The word of God says nothing can separate us from the love of God. Romans 8:38–39 (AMP) says, "For I am convinced and continue to be convinced—beyond any doubt that neither death, nor life, nor angels, nor principalities, nor things present and threatening, nor things to come, nor powers, nor height, nor depth, nor any other created thing, will be able to separate us from the unlimited love of God, which is in Christ Jesus our Lord."

God must be revealed to you. God reveals Himself to His children. You want God to reveal Himself and His will for your life. You must be in constant pursuit of this mission. Jesus Christ died and rose again for every emotional trauma that you've experienced, and you will face. He died for every sadness, depression, confusion, and anxiety that you might be experiencing. You can be freed from faking it, from performing for others to accept you, and from comparing yourself to others, and a lot more. God is all you need, and the sooner you get that revelation the more joy you will have.

You can't do it on your own. You need the Holy Spirit to assist you in getting your deliverance. You can't remove the shame of your past. I know that I couldn't. You can't remove the lies, the fakeness, the regrets, but God can! The gospel is the goodness of God's grace. God will deliver you from internal and external issues that are bombarding your mind and atmosphere. God has given you authority and God has given you His grace and His righteousness.

He Waits for You

Yes, you see, we don't deserve His favor. But God loves us so much that He was willing to let His only Son died such a shameful and humiliating death just so we can be free. "Seeing that we never merit His favor, we are always indebted to Him to extend to us His Mercy and bestow upon us His grace whereby we may respond to Him in an acceptable manner. From beginning to end we are dependent upon Him, for life itself, for all sustenance." I love this song that Travis Green, "You Waited." My favorite part of the song is

> And You, you waited for me, just for me
> You waited for me, just for me
>
> Where would I be, if You left me, God?
> Where would I be, if You left me, God?
> Where would I be, if You left me, God?
> Where would I be, if You left me, God?

The thing is some people will never give the credit to who truly deserves it—God. But I give all the glory to God. He knew my past. God saw my shame, horrible sins, hatred, unforgiveness, guilt, and regret. But yet, He still saved my soul from hell. God snatched me from the clutches of Satan and hell. He renewed my mind and changed my stony heart from becoming more callous to a heart filled with love and passion to help others get back their joy.

Some of you are suffering in silence and hurt and can't find one person you can express your pain to. You're struggling but can't share it with anyone. You're fallen but have to continue to live a facade. You're weak and have to act like you're strong.

But God's grace says, "No. There is no pretense with me. I can handle your shortcomings. You can be vulnerable with me. I can keep your secrets and your doubts and fears. I can handle your pain, and I am the only one that can heal you completely emotionally and psychologically." The word of God says in 2 Corinthians 12:9, "And He said unto me, my grace is sufficient for thee: for My strength is made perfect in weakness. Most gladly therefore will I rather glory in my infirmities, that the power of Christ may rest upon me."

The Love of Your Church Family
One of the most important things to have is a good church family. My church family was always praying for me. God's grace will keep you while you're in the darkest places of your life. I just want to thank God for surrounding me with people that have been a blessing in my life. I remember there was a season that I was going to the hospital every other week, and I thank God for my Pastor who kept me in prayer and prayed for the spirit of infirmity to be broken off my life. I also thank God for Minister Snovia Danville, who countlessly took me to the hospital always she was there for me, and I am so grateful for God placing her in my life. Some nights, it would be 2 o'clock in the morning and I felt so sick, and she would come over to my house and take me to the hospital. She was always patient and kind, and I was so grateful. God's grace kept me. Thank God for Missionary Smith for always knowing when to check in, I am so grateful for the leaders in my church that keeps me in prayer.

There was one night that I was with my Pastor and I felt so bad, I had to be rushed to the hospital. When I was in the emergency room, the doctor came into the room to assess me. I felt myself going somewhere else. I was floating. I literally left my body and the voices seemed that they were getting farther away. I heard "Come back! Come back!" That is why I could never forget what God used my Pastor and Minister to do that night. I felt the spirit of death, and I knew that I left my body, but God's grace and mercy kept me.

I have been through some severe physical and psychological warfare, but God has kept me. I am determined to fight the good fight of faith. I now know my assignments. One of them is to expose the spirit of depression, psychological torment, and fear, and the second to let you know that you can have joy in your life in abundance through Christ.

I leave with you Psalm 46:10: "Be still and know that I am God; I will be exalted among the heathens, I will be the earth." Don't let anything keep you from making it into heaven. We are living to live again an eternal life that has been promised to us. You have an eternal promise from God, and it is worth fighting for.

Chapter 11:
Don't Quit on Your Joy

It's Time to release and let it go

I once read that "Difficult roads often lead to beautiful destinations, so don't quit."

For two years I struggled with the spirit of depression and was constantly in prayer fighting to keep my joy. The spirit of depression and frustration was doing a number on my mind and my spirit. I was tired of being in the rut, feeling cast down, and I wanted the cycle to end. After God delivered me from the spirit of depression, I made the decision to laugh often, give thanks, surround myself with people that make me laugh loudly, love people even if they are sometimes unlovable, forgive quickly, go afterGod passionately. Dream big and be intentional with who is around me. You see a basic element of a narrative, or story, is the point from which the action is viewed. Your story is being told by the true narrator who is God Almighty, and the narrative of your life must be told by God alone because one of the main advantages of a narrator is that the narrator can see everything. While the readers must flip the pages to see what happens next, the narrator on the other hand knows the pitfalls, the suspense and most importantly he knows how the story will end. Aren't you tired of trying to write your own story, when God has the perfect script for your life? I would encourage you to trust the narrator of your life who is Jesus. Trust the story that is already written out in heaven and ask God to help have enough faith to believe that He is working it out for your good.

In this book, we've discussed how to release toxic thoughts and emotions and how to get yourself out of unhealthy environments and relationships. We've talked about the importance of not holding onto thoughts of unforgiveness and revenge. And we've asked the Holy Spirit to remove thoughts of anger, strife, and negative words that you spoke over yourself and negative words that have been spoken over your life. We've decided to let it go—today, this very second, and this very hour.

Now, you need to decide to keep fighting—don't quit on your joy. Keep on fighting and keep on pressing until you come out of depression—until you come out of *oppression*—and keep fighting until you take back everything that the devil has stolen from you. Your feelings are valid to God.

I remember that I was going through a hard patch and one of my friends said, "Oh, you just have to get over it." I knew that they meant well and didn't want to continue to see me suffer so much pain and heartache, but I couldn't get through it without the holy presence of God sweeping over my soul and renewing my mind. I thank God when He removed the hurt and the pain that I was feeling during that season of my life.

Our hope, peace, and joy are in Christ Jesus. The Bible clearly states that He is the author and finisher of our faith. You can trust Him with your failures, weaknesses, and shortcomings. He is the ancient of days, just like a songwriter called Him, which simply means that God never changes, He is the same yesterday, today and forever. You are enough today, you were enough yesterday, and you will definitely be enough tomorrow. Stop talking about your problems and start talking about your joy. Pray that God will bring people in your life that don't have a problem celebrating with you as you experience God's joy. Always remember that joy is one of the most magnetic forces in the universe.

Here are some people that didn't stop fighting but had tons of opportunities and reasons to quit or give up. They refused to settle for less; they kept on fighting for their dreams, and so can you.

Nelson Mandela
[54]Nelson Mandela was a famous African American man who I admire a lot. Nelson Mandela spent twenty-seven years as a political prisoner. He became a leader among his fellow inmates, fighting for better treatment, better food, and study privileges. He earned a bachelor's degree through a correspondence course while being imprisoned. He also became a symbol of hope and anti-apartheid resistance for his entire country. While behind bars, he continued to build his reputation as a political leader, refusing to compromise his beliefs to gain freedom, and upon his release, he led negotiations that resulted in the democracy he had always fought for. Although he was physically bound, his spirit and mind were free.

He was elected president of South Africa and received more than 250 awards, including the Nobel Peace Prize. His funeral was a global event. He could have decided to lie low, give in, and let those twenty-seven years sap his motivation and influence. It would have been easy enough. But he didn't stop fighting and you shouldn't either.

Helen Keller
[55]Helen Keller was an author, lecturer, and crusader for the handicapped. Born in Tuscumbia, Alabama, Keller lost her sight and hearing at the age of nineteen months to an illness now believed to have been scarlet fever. Five years later, on the advice of Alexander

Graham Bell, her parents applied to the Perkins Institute for the Blind in Boston for a teacher, and from that school, they hired Anne Mansfield Sullivan. Keller learned from Sullivan how to read and write in Braille and how to use the hand signals of the deaf-mute. Through Sullivan's extraordinary instructions, the little girl learned to understand and communicate with the world around her.

She went on to acquire an excellent education. Her later efforts to learn how to speak were less successful, and in her public appearances. She required the the assistance of an interpreter to make herself understood. Her impact as an educator, organizer, and fundraiser was enormous, and she became an important influence on the treatment of the blind and deaf. She was responsible for many advances in public services to the handicapped. No one would have faulted her for living a quiet life of solitude, given her seemingly insurmountable disability. But she didn't.

Beethoven
[56]Beethoven was a famous artist who faced several challenges in his life from a very young age. You see, Beethoven endured many significant hardships. He lost his loving mother before age seventeen. From an early age, he was forced to assume increasing responsibility for the household due to his father's heavy drinking. By his late twenties, he was already starting to lose his hearing. Beethoven began to lose his learning at the height of his career and eventually became completely deaf. He sawed the legs off his piano so he could set it on the floor and feel the vibrations as he played. His "Symphony No. 9," of which he never heard a single note, is one of the best-known works of classical music. He could have given in to the suicidal thoughts that overtook him at first and become just another poetic tragedy. But he didn't give up and you shouldn't neither.

Elie Wiesel and Viktor Frankl

[57]Elie Wiesel and Viktor Frankl experienced the unspeakable heroes of the Nazi concentration camps. Elie Wiesel went on to spread a message of hope, atonement, and peace, drawing from his struggles to come to terms with the presence of evil in the world. He wrote over forty books, including the acclaimed memoir *Night*, and he was a political activist for human justice, tolerance, and freedom the world over. He was awarded the Nobel Peace Prize for his crusades for human dignity. He could have become disillusioned, bitter, and withdrawn from the world. Few of us would have faulted him for that. But he didn't.

From his attempts to find a reason to keep living amid daily suffering, Viktor Frankl developed a philosophy that even in the most hopeless situation, man can find internal meaning and purpose. He taught that even when we are helpless to change our circumstances, we have within us the power to summon the will to live. He pioneered existential and humanist psychiatric systems and wrote more than thirty-two books, including his hallmark *Man's Search for Meaning*. He could have been broken and defeated by the horrors he experienced. Most of us probably would have done the same in his situation. But he didn't give up and you shouldn't neither.

Albert Einstein, Alexander Graham Bell, Leonardo da Vinci, Thomas Edison, Walt Disney, and Winston Churchill

All these famous individuals are said to have displayed signs of learning disabilities, like dyslexia. They did poorly in school. They were called stupid, talentless, unteachable, and that they would never amount to anything beyond ordinary. I'm sure you know that they all went on against the odds to do some extremely impressive things. They could have believed the negative voices and been the smallest versions of themselves. But they didn't.

Speaking of Thomas Edison, in addition to failing about ten thousand times before landing on a successful design for the light bulb ("I have not failed; I've just found 10,000 ways that won't work"), his factory burned to the ground when he was sixty-seven, destroying countless lab records and millions of dollars of equipment. When he surveyed his losses, he made the remark, "There is great value in disaster. All our mistakes are burned up. Thank God we can start anew." He could have thrown in the towel at any one of these setbacks. It certainly seemed like "fate" was trying to tell him to do so. But he didn't give up on his dream and you should keep pursuing your dreams.

Jackie Joyner-Kersee
Jackie Joyner-Kersee was diagnosed with asthma when she was eighteen. She is now a six-time Olympic medalist in track and field, she is ranked among the all-time greatest athletes in the women's heptathlon and was named by Sports Illustrated for Women as the Greatest Female Athlete of the Twentieth Century. She could have seen herself as defective or weak and given up on her dreams. But she didn't. Here are a few quotes that she's has said that are encouraging for you to never give up:
- "The medals don't mean anything, and the glory doesn't last. ..."
- "Once I leave this earth, I know I've done something that will continue to help others." ...
- "Ask any athlete: We all hurt at times."

As we can see she didn't allow physical restraints to stop her, and you shouldn't neither.

Go Big or Go Home!
Give God your best—your best in time, talent, and efforts. This has been my motto, and determination in life. Serve Him with

your whole heart. We serve a big God that can do big things in our lives. You just need to believe it. If you're going to invest, invest in your calling, the divine purpose of God in your life.

You see, when I got saved, I knew that I fell in love with God, and I wanted to serve Him. Once I realized that God had a calling on my life, I began to invest my time in studying the word, and I had a strong desire to go to Bible college. It was one of the best decisions that I have made. I learned so much and enjoyed the experience. There were times where I felt tired, felt like giving up, but I knew that it was in the will of God and God gave me the grace to complete it to the end.

You must be fully committed and dedicated to receiving everything that God has for your life. When my Pastor asked me to go to Jamaica to help out with the work that God called her to start in Jamaica, I realized that when I told God nearly twenty years ago, "Where you lead me, I will follow," was really being put to the test. I was nervous, but I had this peace that I was doing exactly what I was meant to do on this earth, and that was to serve God's people. It brings me joy to teach people about the love of God and share the Gospel of Jesus Christ. You might not have been given the best start in life, or even the best circumstances, but you are loved by God.

Know the Story God Has Written for You
There are usually three stories that are told: the story that you tell about yourself, the story that people say about you, and lastly, the story that God has written before the creation of this world about you.

Knowing Christ has delivered me from the way people influenced me and how I see myself, I've become comfortable with being who God has called me to be. I have chosen to focus and find out the story that God has formulated for my life.

Sometimes, we put a period in our story where God has placed a comma. Why? Because your story is not over. Years ago, things got so rough that I had to sleep in my car because I thought someone who I thought was a friend would take me in, but she didn't. In that season, I felt alone and hopeless, but God was with me. He was there to shield and prevent me from being another episode of *Criminal Minds*. At that time, I didn't know how I was going to make it, I had given up on myself, but I thank God that the Lord never gave up on me. So yes, you may be facing some challenges and hard times, but you are stronger than you think. Greater is He that is in you than He that is in the world. You are going to make it! God is able to take care of the situation.

How do you learn about the story God has for us? You can read the word of God, staying in His presence, and praying. Everyone has an incredible story, and we can only discover that story by exploring the will of God through His word. The decisions that we make today will determine our story.

Often, we make a permanent decision at a temporary rest stop. A rest stop is a place for us to recharge, refresh, and get ready to move forward; it was never designed as a permanent place for us to stay. Take your life out of autopilot and start living. You are created for more than just to get up, go to work, come back, have your dinner, go to bed, and do the same thing the next day.

Live Your Life with Purpose and Passion
Live your life with purpose and passion. Have a passion for what you do in the gifts and talents that God has placed upon your life. You will find joy in being in the center of God's will, and as you begin to seek Him, He will reveal His purpose for your life. Don't forget to stay in that "secret place" that is mentioned in Psalms. You must be intentional in your pursuit of maintaining God's joy. That thing that you are obsessed with, the things that you want

to fix, or the things that are your burden, are usually your calling. When you do things that you are passionate about, it will bring you joy. The word of God says in Hebrews 12:2-3 2 "...looking unto Jesus, the author and finisher of our faith, who for the joy that was set before Him endured the cross, despising the shame, and has sat down at the right hand of the throne of God. For consider Him who endured such hostility from sinners against Himself, lest you become weary and discouraged in your souls."

Take me, for example.I love God, I love people, and I love serving others. As I shared with you earlier, I found my passion. No one had to force me. I served with joy and I looked forward to doing it every day. Serving brings me joy. Fuel your passion with prayer and seek instruction and direction from the Lord. Once you seek God, ask Him for guidance, He will put the right people in your life and create opportunities for your gift to build His kingdom. Be the best you, be authentic, be genuine, and be true to God and yourself. Stop doubting and stop procrastinating. Just do it, like Nike says! Actually, Nike wasn't the first to come up with this concept but in the word of God is says in 1 Thessalonian 5:24 " Faithful is he that calleth you, who also will do it." You can depend on God, that no matter what He is faithful to His children.

The Lord is shaping us for eternity, for the Eternal Savior is longing to prepare His children to meet Him someday. There is absolutely nothing that you can keep away from God; He knows it all. Our afflictions, our shortcomings, our bad habits, or our sinful tendencies, our God is aware of it all. He knows when you are sad, when you need to be comforted, when you are feeling low, when you've lost your joy, and most of all when you've reached your lowest point. Your eternity, being secure in God, should bring you joy and peace.

I believe that as long as there is breath in our lungs, there is hope! Jesus is your hope and joy. So, get up and Push yourself even when you don't feel like it. Get up and get back in the ring because Jesus is right there fighting for you and you are a winner!

Write down five things that you're doing to start today to maintain your Joy:

1. _____
2. _____
3. _____
4. _____
5. _____

Endnotes

1. National Institute of Mental Health. "Depression."https://www.nimh.nih.gov/health/topics/depression/index.shtml

2. (*King James Bible*, 1769/n.d., John 10:10) King James Bible. (n.d.). King James Bible Online. https://www.kingjamesbibleonline.org/ (Original work published 1769)

3. (*King James Bible*, 1769/n.d., John 10:10) King James Bible. (n.d.). King James Bible Online. https://www.kingjamesbibleonline.org/ (Original work published 1769)

4. National Institute of Mental Health. https://www.nimh.nih.gov/health/topics/depression

5. (King James Bible, 1769/n.d., II Corinthians 10:4-5) King James Bible. (n.d.). King James Bible Online. https://www.kingjamesbibleonline.org/ (Original work published 1769)

6. (King James Bible, 1769/n.d., John 10:27 28) King James Bible. (n.d.). King James Bible Online. https://www.kingjamesbibleonline.org/ (Original work published 1769)

7. King James Bible, 1769/n.d., Isaiah 41:10) King James Bible. (n.d.). King James Bible Online. https://www.kingjamesbibleonline.org/ (Original work published 1769)

8   Scofield, C. I., & Rikkers, D. W. (2003). The Scofield study Bible: King James version. New York: Oxford University Press.

9   King James Bible, 1769/n.d., Jeremiah 1:5) King James Bible. (n.d.). King James Bible Online. https://www.kingjamesbibleonline.org/ (Original work published 1769)

10 King James Bible, 1769/n.d., Mark 4:35-41) King James Bible. (n.d.). King James Bible Online. https://www.kingjamesbibleonline.org/ (Original work published 1769)

11 King James Bible, 1769/n.d., I Kings 19) King James Bible. (n.d.). King James Bible Online. https://www.kingjamesbibleonline.org/ (Original work published 1769)

12 (King James Bible, 1769/n.d., Genesis 1:3) King James Bible. (n.d.). King James Bible Online. https://www.kingjamesbibleonline.org/ (Original work published 1769)

13 King James Bible, 1769/n.d., 1 John 4:4) King James Bible. (n.d.). King James Bible Online. https://www.kingjamesbibleonline.org/ (Original work published 1769)

14 Merriam-Webster. (n.d.). Semantics. In Merriam-Webster.com dictionary. Retrieved January 4, 2020, from page 117)

15 Merriam-Webster. (n.d.). Semantics. In Merriam-Webster.com dictionary. Retrieved January 4, 2020, from page 123)

16 (King James Bible, 1769/n.d., Ephesians 3:20) King James Bible. (n.d.). King James Bible Online. https://www.kingjamesbibleonline.org/ (Original work published 1769)

17 (King James Bible, 1769/n.d., Psalms 68:5) King James Bible. (n.d.). King James Bible Online. https://www.kingjamesbibleonline.org/ (Original work published 1769)

18 (King James Bible, 1769/n.d., James 2:17-20) King James Bible. (n.d.). King James Bible Online. https://www.kingjamesbibleonline.org/ (Original work published 1769)

19 (King James Bible, 1769/n.d., 1 Kings 18:16-39) King James Bible. (n.d.). King James Bible Online. https://www.kingjamesbibleonline.org/ (Original work published 1769)

20 www.tamarakulish.com, March 2018

21 Maclaren, A. (1900). Expositions of Holy Scripture. London, England: Hodder & Stoughton

22 Maclaren, Alexander. *Paul's Epistle to the Romans, Volume 24; Volume 1909,*

23 Maclaren, A. (1900). Expositions of Holy Scripture. London, England: Hodder & Stoughton

24 C.S. Lewis, <u>Letters to Malcolm: Chiefly on Prayer</u>. San Diego: Harvest, 1964, 92–93.

25 Robert Lowry., The United Methodist Hymnal. 362 "<u>Nothing But the Blood</u>"

26 C.S. Lewis, <u>Letters to Malcolm: Chiefly on Prayer</u>. San Diego: Harvest, 1964, 92–93.

27 Smallwood, David. Who Says I'm an Addict: <u>A Book for Anyone Who Is Partial to Food, Sex, Booze or Drugs</u>. London: Hay House, 2014.

28 Merriam-Webster. (n.d.). Semantics. In Merriam-Webster.com dictionary. Retrieved January 4, 2020, from page 117)

29 James Strong, *Strong's Dictionary of the Bible*, 2,603.

30 Zodhiates, S., & Strong, J. (1991). The complete word study New Testament: King James Version. Chattanooga, TN: AMG Publishers.

31 Stott, J. R. W. (1999). *Basic Christianity*. Grand Rapids: Eerdmans.

32 (King James Bible, 1769/n.d., 1 Kings 18:16-39) King James Bible. (n.d.). King James Bible Online. https://www.kingjamesbibleonline.org/ (Original work published 1769)

33 Smith, Al. Al Smith's Treasury of Hymn Histories. Better Music Publications, 1985.

34 Smith, Al. Al Smith's Treasury of Hymn Histories. Better Music Publications, 1985.

35 Charles Spurgeon, *The Complete Works of C. H. Spurgeon, Volume 9: Sermons 487 to 546*

36 Charles Spurgeon, The Complete Works of C. H. Spurgeon, Volume 9: Sermons 487 to 546

37 Jon Courson's Application Commentary, Nashville, Tenn. : Thomas Nelson Publishers, c2003.

38 https://www.mayoclinic.org/diseases-conditions/panic-attacks/symptoms-causes/syc-20376021

39 https://www.mayoclinic.org/diseases-conditions/panic-attacks/symptoms-causes/syc-20376021

40 Charles Spurgeon, *The Complete Works of C. H. Spurgeon, Volume 9: Sermons 490 to 555*

41 Charles Spurgeon, *The Complete Works of C. H. Spurgeon, Volume 9: Sermons 230 to 330*

42 Charles Spurgeon, *The Complete Works of C. H. Spurgeon, Volume 9: Sermons 487 to 546*

43 https://nickwignall.com/self-sabotage/

44 https://nickwignall.com/self-sabotage/

45 King James Bible, 1769/n.d., James 2:20) King James Bible. (n.d.). King James Bible Online. https://www.kingjamesbibleonline.org/ (Original work published 1769)

46 https://www.runnersworld.com/runners-stories/a27469714/gabriele-grunewald-american-runner/

47 Tozer, A. W. (1961). The knowledge of the holy: **The Attributes of God**: Their Meaning in the Christian Life.

48 Frankl, V. E. 1. (1984). Man's search for meaning: an introduction to logotherapy. 3rd ed. New York: Simon & Schuster

49 Merriam-Webster. (n.d.). Semantics. In Merriam-Webster.com dictionary. Retrieved January 4, 2020, from page 120)

50 Merriam-Webster. (n.d.). Semantics. In Merriam-Webster.com dictionary. Retrieved January 4, 2020, from page 133)

51 (King James Bible, 1769/n.d., Genesis 15:16-17) King James Bible. (n.d.). King James Bible Online. https://www.kingjamesbibleonline.org/ (Original work published 1769)

52 James Strong, *Strong's Dictionary of the Bible*, 2,603.

53 Goodrick, E. W., & Kohlberger, J. R., III. (2004). Mount. The Strongest NIV Exhaustive Concordance (pp. 768-769). Zondervan.

54 Meredith, M. (1998). *Nelson Mandela: A biography*. New York: St. Martin' Press

55 Keller, H. (1954). The story of my life. Garden City, N.Y.: Doubleday.

56 Sullivan, J. W. N. 1. (1960-1927). Beethoven: <u>His Spiritual Development</u>. New York: Vintage.

57 Frankl, V. E. 1. (1984). Man's search for meaning: an introduction to logotherapy. 3rd ed. New York: Simon & Schuster.

CPSIA information can be obtained
at www.ICGtesting.com
Printed in the USA
BVHW031417051021
618195BV00001B/9